Do any of the following sound familiar?

- You expect your kids to act up, and they more than fulfill your expectations.
- Buy your kid one thing and an instant later he wants the next latest and greatest do-wacka-do.
- Anything you say turns into an argument, and you are the one who feels bad.
- Even Einstein couldn't count the number of eye-rolls you've seen.
- Your daughter knows exactly where your guilt button is and when to push it.
- Your son calls to tell you where he is, only he's somewhere else.
- If you hear "whatever" one more time, you'll FedEx your daughter one way to Uganda.
- Your kids don't pay attention until you've called their names three times, each time with a little more velocity.
- She's the poster child for "It's all about me."
- Peer-pack mentality wins hands down over common sense and family values.
- He complains when you haven't had time to do his homework.
- You wish she could spell the word *grateful*, much less act like it once in a while.
- You're trying to do your best, but it's never good enough.
- Your kid's mouth is busier than she is . . . and not in a good way.
- He's never wrong. And when he is, it's someone else's fault.
- Your kids don't even bother with excuses. They do whatever they want.

- He just told you his self-esteem is in the toilet because of you.
- If her jeans don't cost at least a Benjamin Franklin, she won't wear them.
- Your daily parenting mantra is "Expect nothing and you won't be disappointed."
- Ask her to take out the trash and the world as you know it ends.
- "I want," "But you have to," and "You better, or else" are household phrases.
- The last time she thought about helping someone else out was, well, never.
- Your kids are allergic to visiting their grandparents.
- You spend more time saying, "If you ever do that again, I'll . . ." than hugging your kids.
- The last family meal you had without someone whining, arguing, or leaving the table in a huff was . . . the Ice Age.
- The word *sacrifice* is as foreign as the concept of *picking up after oneself*.
- Only one family member respects your authority—the dog.

Parents everywhere face the same issues. We all want to raise kids with character instead of kids who are characters, but we often don't get quite what we expect. However, there is a way to rear a successful child in today's entitled world, a son or daughter who will wisely and confidently blaze a unique trail into adulthood. But the secret of that success starts with you, parent. No one else will do.

Want children who are patient and kind, humble and thankful, and respectful of you, themselves, and others? Who have a hard-work ethic, not giving up until a job is done, even if others say it's impossible? Who succeed in all areas of life—personally, professionally, and relationally—to the best of their ability?

You can't force your kids to be grateful for everything you do, but you can raise successful kids with a healthy self-image and good doses of responsibility and accountability. These children will grow into adults you can be proud of and who stay even-keeled in life's stormy seas, even acting as ship captains for others.

There's a bonus too. Down the road, those children will want to return home to you, with perhaps a partner or a cherub or two in tow. Then, oh, the rollicking stories you can tell to your grandkids around that family dinner table.

Trust me, I know. I've got five kids and four grandkids circulating in and out of my beloved Sande's and my home in Arizona, livening up the atmosphere. It doesn't need to be a holiday, a birthday, or any special occasion for them to return home. They come just because they can and they want to.

So keep turning the pages of this book. It is possible to raise a successful child in a "whatever" generation.

I guarantee it.

8 SECRETS TO RAISING SUCCESSFUL KIDS

8 SECRETS TO RAISING SUCCESSFUL KIDS

NURTURING CHARACTER, RESPECT, AND A WINNING ATTITUDE

DR. KEVIN LEMAN

Revell

a division of Baker Publishing Group
Grand Rapids, Michigan

© 2021 by KAL Enterprises, Inc.

Published by Revell
a division of Baker Publishing Group
PO Box 6287, Grand Rapids, MI 49516-6287
www.revellbooks.com

Printed in the United States of America

Library of Congress Cataloging-in-Publication Data
Names: Leman, Kevin, author.
Title: 8 secrets to raising successful kids : nurturing character, respect, and a winning attitude / Dr. Kevin Leman.
Other titles: Eight secrets to raising successful kids
Description: Grand Rapids : Revell, a division of Baker Publishing Group, 2021.
Identifiers: LCCN 2020051563 (print) | LCCN 2020051564 (ebook) | ISBN 9780800734695 (cloth) | ISBN 9780800740122 (paperback) | ISBN 9781493430499 (ebook)
Subjects: LCSH: Parenting. | Parent and child.
Classification: LCC HQ755.8 .L446 2021 (print) | LCC HQ755.8 (ebook) | DDC 306.874—dc23
LC record available at https://lccn.loc.gov/2020051563
LC ebook record available at https://lccn.loc.gov/2020051564

To protect the privacy of those who have shared their stories with the author, some details and names have been changed.

21 22 23 24 25 26 27   7 6 5 4 3 2 1

To my five grown-up kids,
Holly, Krissy, Kevin II, Hannah, and Lauren.

Your successful lives and love for family prove
that these parenting techniques not only work
but work exceedingly well.

CONTENTS

Acknowledgments   13

Introduction: Raising a Kid with Character, Not One Who Is
a Character   15
Eight time-tested strategies for success.

STRATEGY #1 **START WITH THE END IN MIND   23**
To get to your goal, you first have to know your target.

STRATEGY #2 **EXPECT THE BEST, GET THE BEST   37**
*How to build character and fine-tune behavior in your little
(and big) characters.*

STRATEGY #3 **GIVE AND YOU SHALL RECEIVE   71**
*How respect and a winning attitude powerfully unleash your
child's motivation.*

STRATEGY #4 **ROLE-MODEL A DISCIPLINED LIFE   108**
*Why you, and only you, are the hero or heroine your child
craves.*

STRATEGY #5 **DISCIPLINE, DON'T PUNISH   131**
*Why reality discipline rocks, punishment ruins, and the three
Cs rule every time.*

STRATEGY #6 **STAY THE COURSE   162**
Six "must" principles for sane parents to live by.

STRATEGY #7 MINIMIZE FRICTION, OPTIMIZE SOLUTIONS 179
How you can get your kids to listen every time.

STRATEGY #8 KEEP THE RELATIONSHIP FIRST, ALWAYS 213
They don't care what you know until they know that you care.

Conclusion: Paying It Forward 231
  Why your legacy of success keeps on giving.

Bonus Section: Especially for Blended-Family Parents 235
  Three big mistakes to avoid so you can blend instead of puree.

A Parent's Top 8 Winning Plays 241

Notes 243

About Dr. Kevin Leman 245

Resources by Dr. Kevin Leman 247

ACKNOWLEDGMENTS

Grateful thanks to:

My multifaceted Revell team.
My longtime editor Ramona Cramer Tucker.

INTRODUCTION

*Raising a Kid with Character, Not One
Who Is a Character*

> Eight time-tested strategies for success.

Imagine this scene.

You arrive home exhausted after finishing a huge work project. Your 11-year-old son and 14-year-old daughter are in the kitchen.

"Let me get that for you, Mom. That looks heavy." Your son sprints toward you to take your bag of groceries, sets it on the counter, and starts putting the food away in the fridge and pantry.

"I knew you'd be beat tonight, so I'm making spaghetti. It's the least I can do since you went grocery shopping for us after your long day," your daughter says. She turns from the stove, a smudge of red sauce on her cheek, to give you a hug.

"Uh, sis, you're wearing some of our dinner," your son jokes and flicks the sauce off his sister's cheek with a dish towel.

She laughs. "Thanks."

"Oh, and we remembered it's Grandma's birthday tomorrow," your son says.

"We ordered her some flowers. Her favorite, roses," your daughter adds.

"Go relax, Mom. We got this." Your son grins. "I'll even clean up her mess." He nods toward his sister.

Your daughter lovingly herds you out of the kitchen and down the hallway. "I'll call you when dinner's ready."

I know the first thing many of you would do. You'd exit that home in a befuddled state, stare at the number on the door, and wonder, *Is this really my house?*

Where are these children? Children who respect their parent, pitch in to help, get along with their siblings, and even think about Grandma?

Such welcome-home scenes and the kids in them don't have to exist only in your dreams. I know, because my five grown-up kids were just like that and still are every time they return home. You too can get such children at your home address by using the time-tested techniques in this book. They've already helped hundreds of thousands of families. They can transform your home and family too.

One Kid with Character Coming Right Up

It's tough these days to raise a kid with character who isn't a character. I ought to know, because *I* was a character who ran my saintly mama ragged. She had two other children who were stars—my straight-A older sister and my athletic, captain-of-the-team older brother. Me? I was the troublesome clown who was always up to something. That's why Mama Leman spent far more hours in the principal's office than I did (which is saying plenty) and even more on her knees every morning on my behalf.

Like the son in the scenario you just read, I did dishes too. Only I didn't *offer* to do them. When dishes were my assigned chore on the list, I did them with a signature twist.

A food-encrusted pot too difficult to clean? Squeeze some soap on it, pour on hot water, and then . . . hide it in the oven. I knew it wouldn't be long before my mom or sister would come along and need that very dish. They'd sleuth out the hiding spot, roll their eyes at yet another antic of mine, and wash the dish themselves.

I don't think it entered their craniums to hold me accountable for my actions or, in this case, my lack of finishing the job. If it did, they knew it would take more energy to chase me down and force me to clean that dish than to do it themselves. So they sighed and cleaned the pot, and life for me went on as usual.

Meanwhile, I'd be out fishing at the local creek, wrestling with my buddy Moonhead, or hiding around the kitchen corner, laughing as they searched for that dish.

Yet through all my antics, my mom never gave up on me. She did all in her power to help this character become somebody who could and would give back to the world. I'm thankful that she lived long enough to see that happen. My "perfect" sister, Sally, whom I annoyed nonstop as a child, now still likes me enough to visit and bring her delectable raspberry pie she's fine-tuned into a masterpiece.

But you don't have to wait decades to get a kid who

- says "please" and "thank you" without prompting.
- clears dishes without being asked.
- keeps his space and yours orderly.
- does homework on time, without reminders.
- engages with you in a mutually satisfying conversation.
- pitches in to help without complaining or whining.
- is kind, thoughtful, honest, and a good listener.
- helps those who are less advantaged or bullied.
- is known for her integrity and keeping promises.
- is self-motivated to do his best but able to accept failure and learn from it.

- is a role model for peers rather than being tossed about by the tornadoes of adolescence.
- appreciates the perks of living at home and tells you so.
- actually *likes* his siblings and sticks up for them.
- stands strong against any tailwind, because she knows she can handle it.
- thinks about and actively plans his future.
- treats you with respect, even if she doesn't always agree with your actions.

In today's entitled "whatever" world, how can you raise a child who fits the above descriptions? Who has a healthy self-image and a strong sense of responsibility? Who lovingly balances taking and giving? Who is self-motivated to reach his best potential? Who is respectful, determined, and known for her good character? Who deals positively with tough circumstances? Who has a winning attitude about next steps even when they're thrown his way or life is uncertain? Who knows what she's good at and pursues it wholeheartedly? And who will, a decade or two from now, want to talk to his siblings and parents on the phone and happily head home for Christmas dinner and family birthdays?

Every parent dreams of being the best parent and having the best child.

Then reality intrudes.

If you can't identify with either of those two statements, you're still wearing one of those shiny new parental crowns. Wear it with pride now in the first few days of your kid's arrival in your home. Soon that baby will start to cry because of colic or diaper rash. After long bouts of that at two in the morning, believe me, that crown will get a bit tarnished, and you'll join the rest of us parents on the planet. If you're an adoptive parent or a stepparent of an older child, the initial glow will end the instant that child says, "You can't make me. You're not my real mom [dad]."

Do yourself a favor. Accept right now that there's no such thing as a perfect parent or a perfect kid. That's a self-defeating concept that needs to be purged. You and your child are both uniquely and wonderfully created yet imperfect.

But there's good news too. Without some of those imperfections, life wouldn't be nearly as interesting, would it? I mean, vanilla ice cream is good, and I'd never turn it down, especially if it comes with a warm piece of homemade apple pie. But rocky road ice cream, slathered with hot caramel and hot fudge and topped with a cherry, is even better.

Slide Right into the Driver's Seat

Some of you are hitting the road as newbie parents. You have the opportunity to get on the front end of raising a successful child, so good for you. Many new parents read a host of articles and books about parenting and then apply what I call the "Jell-O Toss" approach. They read everything, extract all the different flavors, and then toss them all together into one gigantic bowl of experimentation. Then, for kicks, they throw that bowl of combined Jell-O flavors at the parenting wall and see what, if anything, sticks.

But you don't have to adopt such a willy-nilly approach. This book reveals eight time-tested parenting strategies for raising your child into a successful adult and positively growing your relationship along the way.

These foundational techniques aren't situational. They work *every time* to positively grow your relationship through all ages and stages. Sure, there will be bumps in the road, detours, and a few off-roading moments where you might catch air and land among a thistle or two. But you and your kids can emerge with good communication skills, respect for each other, and lifelong camaraderie.

Some of you have a passel of young kids. I know instantly who you are because of the bags under your eyes from sleepless nights and the constant "Look at me" demands from chirpy voices. Those precious creatures, shorter than a yardstick, will all too soon become adolescents. Add 80 pounds in weight and a few feet in height, but keep the same behaviors they have now. Would you want those larger-scale critters ruling your house and calling the shots? Or would you like to see a few things change in the interim for their long-term success and your sanity? Now's a great time to employ the strategies in this book. You'll be glad you did.

> These foundational techniques work EVERY TIME to positively grow your relationship through all ages and stages.

Others of you are well into the adolescent or teenage phase with your children. It can be a stressful roller-coaster ride sometimes, but think of the perks: the daily drama is better than anything on Netflix, and it's free of charge. As you consider peer pressure, middle school, high school, and college or career, the principles of this book become even more important. At this stage, there's a bonus: your kids' logic skills have improved, as illogical as they sound sometimes. That's to your benefit in these strategies. But because both they and you have had some years to develop habits that can be hard to break, you may need to be a bit more persistent in carrying out your mission of change.

Some of you have done the best job as parent that you could, but you still couldn't win "Parent of the Year." Life seems stacked against you. Your kid hasn't turned out the way you'd hoped. Well, today is a day to smile. You can choose to carve a new path. It all starts with you, the irreplaceable role model your child needs, craves, and is already watching. This book will show you how to transform your parent-child relationship.

All parents are plunged into on-the-job training. No one can be fully prepared. If someone would have pulled me aside 10 months before Sande and I conceived our firstborn, Holly, and said, "Hey, bucko, you know those five kids you plan on having? Well, you're going to pay over $620,000 dollars to educate them," I would have passed out from the shock. I was making $10,000 a year when Holly was born. Sande and I barely had nickels to rub together. We had no idea, really, what we were getting ourselves into.

For generations, we parents have shaken our heads, wondering, *How are we going to raise this kid, much less make her a contributing member of society down the road?* But we also have an incredible privilege: to show the next generation—who will then impact the generation after that, and so on—what it looks like to be truly successful.

The principles in this book aren't intended as an abracadabra, "do it once and you're done" trick. Instead, they're basic underpinnings that will change the way you think and respond so your child will then think and respond differently. No matter what age your child is, your efforts will produce a win-win relationship that won't stop when she turns 18 and walks out your door to wherever the wind is blowing her next.

But the journey starts with you. Change even a few things about the way you interact with your child, and you'll be amazed at the transformation in both of you. He'll not only start to behave differently; he'll love the new way your home operates . . . even if he doesn't tell you that until he comes home from college with socks he hasn't washed for months.

STRATEGY #1

START WITH THE END IN MIND

To get to your goal, you first have to know your target.

What do you want to be when you grow up?"

Think back a few years. Isn't that the question every adult asked you when you were a child? And didn't it annoy the heck out of you as a teenager when you wished they'd mind their own business?

When I was young, I wanted to be a fireman. I was dying to drive one of those flashy red trucks, spray water sky-high with that big hose, and lay on the horn as I drove through stoplights.

Later, I wanted to be a dentist who could persuade people to open their mouths and say, "Ahhh," and have all those cool shiny tools, like drills, that fixed their teeth when they ate too much candy. If I *had* become one, have mercy on those patients. I'd have—*oops*—extracted a canine instead of a molar since I wasn't very precise with details or big on studying biology.

Many of us dream of and talk about *what* our kid will become—a doctor, a lawyer, an engineer, a teacher, a scientist, the heir who will take over the family business, or the first in the family to attend college. If I asked you right now what type of job you thought your child might have in the future, I bet you could tell me a few options.

What we don't talk about much is *who* our kids will become. Yet who our kids are right now and who we want them to be in the future is the underlying issue, covering 99 percent of the questions that hundreds of thousands of parents all over the US and Canada ask me. Questions like these:

- She's so mouthy all the time. How can I get my child to be more respectful?
- My 15-year-old doesn't seem to care about anyone other than himself. How can I teach him that others matter too? Like his sister and the elderly lady next door who needs help with her groceries or getting her mail?
- My four-year-old daughter throws a lot of tantrums. How can I get her to stop? At home it's annoying, but at the store it's really embarrassing. We live in a small town, and now I hate to go to the grocery store.
- My 11-year-old is so lazy. He never gets anything done, much less does anything on time. He's late to school half the time, and then he yells at me like it's my fault. How can I break that pattern?
- Our four kids fight over the littlest things. How can I get it to stop? Aren't siblings supposed to love and look out for each other?
- "No" is my six-year-old's favorite word. Ask him to do anything and that's his response, like it's preprogrammed. How can I change his behavior? It's getting old really fast.
- When I asked my kid what he wanted to be when he grew up, he just said "Alive" and went back to web surfing. How can I talk about anything with a kid like that?
- How much is too much to give a kid? My husband and I grew up poor, worked hard, and now have a more

comfortable life. But nothing we give our son seems like enough. He always wants more and makes us feel like we're failing as parents if we can't provide it. How much is enough? Too much?

- I grew up with the "It's all for one and one for all" thinking in my family. But my own kids' mantra is more like, "It's all for me and me for myself." How can I turn that around and get some help around here? Like even getting the kitchen cleaned up?

- My daughter hates math. Whenever I try to help her, she cries or gets mad. She says it's too hard and she's just not good at it. How can I help her get through this?

- My three-year-old never wants to eat anything at meals. If we put food on his high chair tray, he just stares at us as he pushes it off the edge. My carpet is a huge mess from the splatters. Finally, we give up and let him go play so we can at least eat in peace. How can we put a stop to such behavior?

- We're worried about our middle-school son. Who he is seems to switch from day to day, depending on the latest trends and what his peers say or do. How can we turn him back into the kid we used to know and who liked hanging out with us?

- My eight-year-old daughter picks on other kids. This is the third time I've had to leave work after a call from her teacher. Even though I ground her for a week every time, she only shrugs and asks if we're going to get her favorite fast food on the way home. Why won't she stop?

- I'm tired of the door slamming in our house. Sometimes it's intentional, when my kids are mad about something. Other times it's just carelessness as they enter or leave our home. Still, the banging sound is the same. How can I put a halt to that headache-inducing activity? It's driving me nuts.

- My daughter majors in socializing and minors in everything else. Her grades certainly reflect that. But if she can't get her grades up, she won't be able to get into college. How can I make her take life more seriously?
- My third son backs off every time anyone challenges him on even the smallest thing. How can I teach him to stand up for himself? He's going to need that to survive among his pack of three brothers, much less in this dog-eat-dog world.
- My older daughter is a straight-A student. Then there's her sister, whose only A is in gym. The rest of her grades are Ds and dipping. How can I motivate her to be more like her older sister?

These are only a few of the common parental concerns in regard to raising a successful child in an entitled world. I bet you have many other questions too. We'll address all of the above situations and more.

But now I'm going to ask *you* a question: who do you want your child to be when he or she grows up?

Imagining Who, Not What

It's impossible to raise a successful kid if you don't know what your end goal is. So I want you to imagine it's 5, 10, 15, or 20 years down the road. Your children are now adults living on their own, with maybe a partner, a child, or both. When your kids walk through that door to have dinner with you, what do you want that reunion to be like? When you talk or text, how would you like those conversations to go? What do you hope their interactions with their family, friends, spouse, or children will be like?

For now, look past any dreams you have for the *what*: the kind of job they'll have, the amount of money and status they'll have, the car they'll drive, the place they'll live, or where they'll vacation.

Those are all veneers—shiny outside layers that others see and that may define their positions within specific societies but don't say much about who your children are at their core.

Instead, think about the *who* you'd like to see in your kids: their character, behavior, attitudes, and values.

Are they:

- honest and straightforward in all things, including paying taxes (as much as we all hate them)?
- kind to others, considering them equal, whether those people graduated from Harvard or work at the local car wash?
- patient with difficult people and events that don't go as planned?
- comfortable with asking for your opinion, yet they still weigh all options and make their own decisions?
- respectful of, supportive of, and faithful to their partner?
- diligent about putting their full effort into whatever work they do?
- positive and balanced, instead of being ruled by anger and resentment over things in the past or present they can't control?
- confident about what they believe in and acting according to those beliefs?
- sensitive toward and accepting of others with different beliefs, backgrounds, and values, even if they don't understand or agree with their actions?
- conscious of saving for a rainy day instead of spending all of their paycheck?
- able to move on after an adverse circumstance, even if it means sitting in the mud awhile to collect themselves before getting back up?

- eager to make unique, beneficial contributions wherever they are able?

Do they:

- combine a spirit of fun with responsibility?
- refuse to give up, even when the going is tough?
- pitch in to help a neighbor with a project, even if it's not their forte?
- take time to listen to and play with their own kids, prioritizing showing up at their events above getting overtime at work?
- balance future planning and living to the fullest in the present?
- give generously of their time and resources to those less fortunate?
- bounce back after a reversal, saying they've learned something and would try things a different way next time?
- treat others and themselves with respect?
- have empathy for those who are struggling and offer help in an appropriate way?
- firmly hold to their values in spite of what others tell them they should do or not do?
- accept responsibility for their actions, even when consequences might be painful, instead of passing the buck?
- have a healthy self-worth, not allowing anyone to beat them down or take advantage of them?
- carefully weigh decisions before acting?
- take the high road instead of the easy way out on a difficult matter?
- know how to say, "I blew it. I'm sorry"?

Take a few minutes to reflect on who you want your kids to be down the road. Scribble your thoughts about their character, behavior, attitude, and values. I'll wait right here until you're done. . . .

Have at least a starting list? You can always add to it later. In fact, I encourage you to do so. Keep it in a private, easy-to-access spot where you and your partner (if you have one) can add notes. But don't post it where the kids can see it, like on the fridge. Keeping that list secret will give you a needed edge of surprise and more maneuvering ability. Why?

Telling or *reminding* kids of the qualities you want them to have is very different from role-modeling such qualities or using natural consequences to do the teaching for you. You don't like to be constantly told what you should be like, do you? Or that you don't meet others' expectations? Neither do your kids. So let's keep that list between us for now.

Perhaps among your list are these seven common qualities that many parents in my seminars have listed as hallmarks of success:

- self-control
- tenacity
- self-worth
- honesty
- patience
- life balance
- kindness

In this book, I'll reveal how you can proactively encourage those qualities in your kids, without lecturing or being pushy.

For those of you who are people of faith, you may have added other character traits from the famous love passage:

Love is patient, love is kind. It does not envy, it does not boast, it is not proud. It does not dishonor others, it is not self-seeking, it is not easily angered, it keeps no record of wrongs. Love does not delight in evil but rejoices with the truth. It always protects, always trusts, always hopes, always perseveres. Love never fails.[1]

Making Your Dream Qualities Come True

Some of you likely have drafted a long list of overall characteristics you want your children to have. You're the detailed planner, the firstborn or only child in the family you grew up in. Making lists and checking them twice is part of your DNA, so this exercise is invigorating.

If you're a middleborn and you have more than one child, you may have divided your list to make sure each child has an equal number of character qualities. You know what it's like to be lumped in with your brothers and sisters and sometimes feel invisible. It makes sense that you want to consider each child carefully as an individual.

If you're a baby of the family, this has likely been a tough exercise. You've gotten up twice to get coffee or a snack, interacted with at least one other person, and then sat down again with a sigh to make a few notes. How do I know? Because I'm a baby of the family, and that's exactly what I'd do if someone asked me to do this kind of exercise. But stick with the task. I promise it will be worth it.

As my late friend Stephen R. Covey stated in *The 7 Habits of Highly Effective People*, if you want to accomplish anything, you need to "begin with the end in mind."[2] That's why this exercise of identifying the dream qualities you want your child to have is a critical foundation. Simply listing *who* you want your child to be is a big first step toward making those qualities a reality.

Think of it this way. If you don't set your destination when you're driving, you'll likely take a lot of detours. Trying to raise a successful child without identifying your end goal is similar.

A mom of five children ages 2 through 15 recently told me, "I really need things to change around my house." For several minutes she expounded on all the things her kids did that drove her crazy, that she had a heavy load at work, and that her husband didn't help out very much.

Finally I gently held up a hand. "Let me ask you: *how* would you like things to change?"

Her shoulders slumped. "I have no idea. I just need them to change!"

Some of you may feel like that tired mom right now. You really want change, but the process of it feels overwhelming. To be honest, you're not quite sure what success in parenting looks like, since you didn't have a good role model for that when you were growing up. You've learned your techniques from trial and error. That's why we're going to take that change you crave step-by-step, and I'll give you lots of practical examples and real-life solutions to follow.

> If you don't set your destination when you're driving, you'll likely take a lot of detours. Trying to raise a successful child without identifying your end goal is similar.

For those of you who grew up with a parent who could spot your flaws from 50 feet away, you'll have no problem keeping your eye on that end goal. You know all too well how to set a goal. But flexibility along the way when circumstances are thrown at you? That's tougher. After all, you're human and your child is human, and sometimes one or both of you won't cooperate with the plan. Yes, you may have some uncomfortable moments along the way. But I assure you, that end goal of rearing a successful child is worth every bit of the journey.

For those of you who want to be your child's best friend, you may vacillate greatly in your decisions to please him or her. Aiming toward producing a successful adult means sticking to your guns in making decisions that adhere to your goals. That child who may be temporarily upset with you now will thank you in the long run, especially when he has a kid who's exactly like him and you've given him a road map to follow.

For those of you who like to wander life's paths without a map or any planning because that's a lot more fun, your kids deserve *intentional* parenting. They need you to make conscious choices based on set values, beliefs, and goals. Kids thrive on routine and knowing what you expect of them. Those things, and your love, are part of your home's safety net in a tumultuous world.

Kids thrive on routine and knowing what you expect of them.

No matter where you are in your parenting journey, you have to know where you're heading to get there. By simply penning your dream qualities list, you've already done the following:

- identified your specific goals in rearing your child into a successful, balanced adult.
- established a standard to measure decisions against. For example, if you do X, does that action get you closer to or farther away from your set goals?
- given yourself concrete reasons for taking specific actions that may be uncomfortable in the short term but advance your endgame.
- gained awareness of the long-term benefits of intentional parenting.

Look how much you've accomplished already, and this is only the first chapter. Go ahead and give yourself a pat on the back.

Inside Every *What* Is a Little Bit of *Who*

As I look back now at what I wanted to be—a fireman and a dentist—I can't help but laugh. Clearly my actual skills weren't in either of those career tracks. But both held hints of who I was then and who I still am today.

I wanted to be the hero who saved the day, got people's attention, and also brought comfort to those in pain. All three of those threads have a lot to do with who I became: a psychologist who unites families grappling with various issues; an entertainer who grabs attention on TV, radio, podcasts, and social media to deliver wit and wisdom that can change relationships; and someone who cares deeply about helping those who struggle with self, parenting, and family matters by providing real, commonsense answers that work every day.

My saintly mama had no idea what I'd become, but she still never stopped believing that who I was at my core was good and unique, and that I'd eventually end up doing and being something good . . . even when all evidence pointed to the contrary.

My academics were so low that I was stuck with the kids who ate paste. If I got bored and the teacher happened to have her back turned, I slithered out of class on my belly like a snake. I slid under pews at church, targeted women who'd taken off their shoes, and switched them, mixing and matching pairs across the sanctuary. When I was supposed to be at youth group, I was . . . well, somewhere else. I drove one teacher out of teaching and likely into a shrink's office.

Then one teacher in high school said to me, "You know, Kevin, with your skills, you could actually do something with your life."

I was stunned. *Skills? I have skills?*

For the first time I realized I might be able to give something unique back to the world because of who I was. While everyone else at school was fixated on curbing my troublesome behavior, that teacher saw who I was at my core—a born entertainer who cared about helping people.

Each of your cubs lives in the same den, but they're clearly different. One wants to be an accountant while another wants to be a ballerina. A third wants to do dirt-track racing. But if you look carefully within the *what* they dream about doing, you'll find hints about *who* they are.

The accountant-to-be puts a high priority on being detailed, methodical, and careful and may take every failure to heart for a long time because he's a perfectionist. He holds himself to a very high standard and doesn't want to let anyone down, much less himself.

The ballerina values performance, music, and being in the spotlight, and her favorite activity even at a young age may be twirling until she gets dizzy. She's a free spirit who loves spending time with others and is highly emotional.

> If you look carefully within the *what* they dream about doing, you'll find hints about *who* they are.

The dirt-track racer is driven by adrenaline rushes, is the most likely to fall out of a tree because he's always hanging in one, and takes a lot of risks out of curiosity to see where they lead.

You can never treat your accountant, ballerina, or dirt-track racer the same. To help each child succeed in life—now and in the future—you start with key character traits you'd like all your kids to have. But then you factor in each child's unique personality and developing skill set.

Every family has at least one child who forces you to pay attention and gets more than his or her share. It may be the only child who whispers so you can barely hear her until you have to stop what you're doing and bend over to listen. It may be the loud, raucous baby of the family who's unaware how exhausting his constant energy is. It may be the drama-queen firstborn who sets the temperature for the whole household. Amid all the excitement, it's usually the middleborn who discovers his best option is to stay out of the line of fire between older and younger siblings, play middleman when he's forced to, and otherwise do his own thing.

That's why it's important to spend one-on-one time getting to know each of your kids. After all, to get to your end goal, you not only have to know what qualities you're aiming for, you have to know who your kids really are. This is easier when they're young and they have more reason to want to hang out with you. Then those animals called *peers* enter the scene, adolescence kicks in, and finally that driver's license is secured, which means you have to work a lot harder to track those kids down.

Every effort you make is worth it, though. Quality time never trumps quantity time with kids. In fact, to get *any* quality time, you have to spend quantity time building four foundations. These foundations for life success—character, behavior, respect, and a winning attitude—and the resulting long-lasting benefits for you and your kids are the subjects of the next two chapters.

As an extra perk, I've sprinkled my "10-Second Solutions" to the hottest questions parents asked (from pages 24–26) throughout the remainder of this book. Think of the hunt as a "mission possible," with each solution being a practical clue to speed you ahead on your mission of rearing a successful child.

"Your mission, parent, should you choose to accept it . . ."

Here's the first clue.

Dr. Leman's 10-Second Solutions

Q: She's so mouthy all the time. How can I get my child to be more respectful?

A: Nothing a little duct tape wouldn't solve. Seriously, when she mouths off, just walk away. Then the next time she wants to go somewhere or do something (which with kids doesn't take long), you and/or that car simply are not available.

When she asks why, say, "I don't appreciate the way you talked to me this morning [or whenever]."

Then comes the hardest part: sticking to your guns. No batting of her baby blues, whining, crying, or angry tirades change the picture. That kid goes nowhere. She has a lot of time to think through her actions, their consequences, and what she'll do differently next time now that she knows Mom or Dad has a backbone of steel.

Case closed.

STRATEGY #2

EXPECT THE BEST, GET THE BEST

How to build character and fine-tune behavior in your little (and big) characters.

My mommy has a lot of jobs," a wise-beyond-her-years four-year-old once told me. "She's my mommy, my daddy's wife, and a worker. No wonder she gets tired and cries. Sometimes she yells too."

Parents, you do have a lot of jobs. As a parent of five kids, I know firsthand that parenting isn't easy. It's filled with challenges you didn't count on and lots of surprises that are fun and, well, not so fun.

Let's admit it right up front. One of your brood is trickier to deal with than the others. But if you build on the four foundations we'll explore in this chapter and the next, not only will you increase your child's potential for success in every area of life, but your parenting journey from here on out will be incredibly rewarding and a lot less stressful.

For some starting inspiration, I want to share a story with you. It's about a girl whose mother always said she was "a little extra."[1] She grew up on the south side of Chicago with her father, mother, and brother, all living in a tiny apartment over a home owned by her great-aunt.

As an ethnic girl from a working-class background, she realized she'd get "tracked early" and put "in a box of underachievement" if she didn't show some star ability.[2] That reality, and seeing her parents' sacrifices—her disabled father put on his shift-worker uniform and went to work every day, and her mother didn't buy clothes for herself—kicked in her drive to succeed and distinguish herself. Eventually her determination and never-give-up spirit won out over her circumstances. That young woman got into an Ivy League university—as did her brother—received her JD at an Ivy League law school, and joined a large firm in her hometown of Chicago.

What made the biggest difference in her life? Her parents' investment in her. Kids know when they're not being invested in, she says. She clearly saw that in her inner-city community: "Failure is a feeling long before it becomes an actual result. It's vulnerability that breeds with self-doubt and then is escalated by fear."[3]

Watching the varying responses of her parents and grandparents to tough circumstances, she realized that what "happens to a person who knows deep inside . . . they are more than what their opportunities allowed them to be" depends significantly on their perspective of life and themselves.[4] For her grandfather, not being able to change his status created a deep discontent that lingered. But her parents focused on experiencing the fullest life possible, including simple rewards of ice cream or pizza for a job well done. They didn't induce guilt that she should strive for more or be more. Instead they gave her freedom to have her own ideas and space to explore them, supported her in whatever she chose to do, and simply expected her to give her best.

"Kids are born into this world with a sense of hope and optimism, no matter where they're from or how tough their stories are," she states, adding that there are no bad kids, only bad circumstances. "They think they can be anything because we tell them that, so we have a responsibility to be optimistic and to operate in the world that way."[5]

That young woman would someday become Michelle Obama, the approachable first lady whose inspiring legacy on behalf of children and families in the US and abroad lives on in multiple arenas even though she's left the White House.[6]

What Her Parents Did Right

Michelle's story is not only inspiring but motivational for parents everywhere. Her parents didn't have an easy life. They lived humbly and worked hard to provide the basics for their children. But they also didn't allow any of the cards they were dealt stop them from doing all they could to unleash their children's potential and motivate them toward success.

What exactly did they do right? Here's the Dr. Leman take: instead of focusing on what they *didn't have*, they focused on what they *could do*.

First, they invested in their children. They knew who their children were at their core from spending time with them. They knew Michelle's character—that she was self-motivated from observing the context around her and didn't need to be pushed. She was already pushing herself hard enough.

> Instead of focusing on what they *didn't have*, they focused on what they *could do*.

Second, their own behavior of plowing ahead, making the best of their circumstances, and never giving up acted as a powerful role model. Working hard was a family trait. They didn't have to tell Michelle to work hard because she saw her parents doing so day in and day out. They didn't play guilt games of "Look at all we're doing for you. You better repay us someday." Nor did they use threats, such as, "If you don't get good grades, you're going to be a failure in life." Instead, they went about their business, letting their actions speak louder than words ever could.

Third, they respected their kids' opinions and ideas and allowed them to freely experiment in whatever they chose to do. They didn't tell their kids what to do.

Fourth, they may not have had a lot of money or material possessions, but they remained optimistic about the future. They chose to highlight hope and achievement and celebrate a job well done as a family.

In short, those smart parents knew their children's *character*, role-modeled successful *behavior*, had *respect* for their children's ideas and distinctiveness, and showcased *a winning attitude* about life. Because they built their relationship on those four foundations, Michelle's parents raised a daughter who was grateful and happy for what she had, who wasn't always looking at the next thing, and whose values didn't change whether she was in that tiny apartment in south Chicago or in the White House. That's because, as Michelle has said, "The House didn't define us, it's the *values* that defined us."[7]

Later in life Michelle would encourage her own two college-bound daughters to "figure out who they want to be in the world, not who they think I want them to be, not what the rest of the world says about them."[8] Doesn't that life mantra sound familiar? Where do you think she got it from?

You're right. Her mom and dad. Their daily role-modeling had a lot to do with it.

Want a child who is grateful and happy for what she has? Whose values don't change no matter where she goes? Who decides who she wants to be instead of letting others define her?

If you want to unleash your child's potential and motivate her toward such success, expect the best and you'll get the best. Build the four foundations for life success into your relationship from today forward.

> ## The Four Foundations for Life Success
>
> Foundation 1: Character
> Foundation 2: Behavior
> Foundation 3: Respect
> Foundation 4: A Winning Attitude

Cultivating Rock-Solid Character in Your Little and Big Characters

If you want a thoughtful, grateful, kind, courteous, respectful child, you have to start with the end in mind. Your child may be a toddler or in elementary school, middle school, or high school. No time is too late to launch a new journey together. From this moment on, you simply need to weave such virtues so tightly into the fabric of your home and family that the fibers can't be extracted. Cultivating rock-solid character in your little and big characters establishes a foundation from which you build acceptable behavior, the two-way street of respect, and a winning attitude about life.

But how exactly *do* you cultivate character in your kids? Let's take a look at the seven common character traits parents wish for their kids, which I listed in Strategy #1:

- self-control
- tenacity
- self-worth
- honesty
- patience

- life balance
- kindness

If you want to produce a child with these character traits, how would you do that?

Self-Control

When a young child has a tantrum, most parents try to talk him out of it. They cajole, "Oh, honey, don't be like that." They threaten, "Stop that this instant." Or they offer treats if he stops. Those methods might halt the behavior once, but they won't work long-term. When a child gets what he wants, he'll continue that behavior. Understanding that isn't rocket science.

If a two-year-old pitches a fit during dinner at home and starts throwing food, holding down his hands might work for that one meal. But here's a better plan. Continue your conversation with whomever you were talking to. Remove the food from the offending toddler's high chair so he can't continue his splatter of artwork. Without a word to him or showing any frustration or anger, nonchalantly pick up the high chair with the toddler in it and move it around the corner, where he can no longer see you. For toddlers, that tiny distance away from Mama seems like a universe away.

Since such behavior is meant to get your attention, removing your child from your space is the best way to help him start developing self-control. That toddler is smarter than you think. *Oh, I get it. If I pitch a fit at dinner and throw food, Mama sticks me around the corner. I don't like it when I can't see Mama. I better not do that again.* Thus, even a toddler can begin to develop self-control through such parental action.

The sooner kids learn that self-control and delayed gratification are a part of life, the better for them, you, and everyone else around them. Children who don't have self-control end up becoming bullies and entitled princess or prince wannabes, and they do whatever they feel like doing, whenever they feel like doing it, to whomever they want. Lack of self-control is a recipe for disaster. They'll lose friends and win a lot of enemies. They'll have a difficult time handling any situation that doesn't go their way and lose job after job.

If your eight-year-old decides to run over your neighbor's flowers with his bike just because he feels like it and thinks it'll be fun, immediate consequences should descend. He doesn't go to his baseball game. Instead, he marches up to that door, with you standing behind him, and apologizes directly to the neighbor for his act. *He* faces the neighbor's wrath, not you. Even better if you know the neighbor, secretly call ahead, and say you are trying to teach a life lesson and would like them to help you out by doing some very good acting. Even a crotchety neighbor would likely be happy to oblige.

Then your son goes home, digs deep into the reserves he was saving for a skateboard, and accompanies you to buy brand-new flowers. He spends the rest of the day digging up the crushed flowers and planting new ones, then cleaning up the mess. His weekend he'd planned is shot, and he's certainly not happy. But he'll never forget that lesson. I bet the next time he rides his bike, he'll give that bank of flowers a wide berth and tell his buddies to stay away from it too.

If your angry 15-year-old punches his fist through your drywall, let him retreat to his room and cool off. But he doesn't go anywhere. He learns how much drywall repair costs, and he funds it out of his own allowance and money he got by mowing yards when he was 12. Even better if he has to attempt the repair job himself with some spackle, sandpaper, and paint. It may not be perfect, but every time he passes that spot in your hallway, believe me, he'll see it. The blemish on the wall and the consequences will be a constant reminder not to lose self-control in that way again.

See how easy this method is? You let the consequences do the loud talking for you and rest up your vocal cords.

Tenacity

If you want a child who doesn't give up easily when faced with adversity, start with baby steps.

Your child is discouraged about his bad grade on a science test. "I'll never learn science. I'm just dumb," he says.

You sit beside him. "Hey, science was tough for me too. I got some grades I wasn't happy with. But you know what? I believe

Dr. Leman's 10-Second Solutions

Q: My four-year-old daughter throws a lot of tantrums. How can I get her to stop? At home it's annoying, but at the store it's really embarrassing. We live in a small town, and now I hate to go to the grocery store.

A: Hold your head high and sashay right past that fit-throwing child flailing on all fours in the aisle. If someone approaches, roll your eyes and say, "Well . . . some people's children." Then whip around the corner just far enough to be out of your cherub's eyesight but still able to keep an eye on her.

After a moment of shock, she'll realize you've disappeared from her sight. In a second she'll be racing around the corner where you "disappeared," saying, "Mama, I'm sorry. I didn't mean it. I love you." It will be a while before she tries that again.

If she throws another fit, you go round two to reinforce your new way of handling that behavior.

If another parent in that store happens to know you, they'll learn something too . . . and think you're awfully clever. They might even try that technique out for themselves.

in you. I know that if you stick to it, you can overcome anything. Even the periodic table of elements. Nothing is going to get you down. You showed that in the past when . . ." You tell him about a time or two when he didn't give up and the situation turned out well.

Note that you don't give him false hope he'll get an A in a subject that is not his natural bent. But such words empower him to do his best, because you already believe in him and expect the best out of him. He may not be the next Einstein, but he doesn't have to be at the bottom of his class either.

If your four-year-old gives up partway through putting her toys away, point that out gently. "I see you put half of your toys away. Thank you. Go ahead and finish putting the rest of them away while I make dinner. After all, you're an Anderson. And we Andersons always finish what we start."

Your high-school senior is overwhelmed by her college options and doesn't even know where to start. You say, "Start by checking out one school. List the pros and cons. Then once you're satisfied you know enough about that school, set it aside and look at the next one. If you look at them one at a time and stick with it, you'll get the job done. You always do. Remember when you were a kid and you . . ." You remind her about the lemonade stand she had that didn't make any money for three days, but she stuck with it for all of her spring break and had earned over a hundred bucks by the end of it.

Such simple and positive techniques, handled in the moment, spur on a child to be tenacious in character, sticking to his tasks until they're completed. He thinks, *Okay, this is hard now, but Mom [Dad] is right. I kept going even when things were tough earlier, and I got the job done. I will this time too.*

Many people give up when the going is hard. If you teach your child tenacity, he or she will emerge clearly as a head above the crowd.

Dr. Leman's 10-Second Solutions

Q: My older daughter is a straight-A student. Then there's her sister, whose only A is in gym. The rest of her grades are Ds and dipping. How can I motivate her to be more like her older sister?

A: She'll never be like her sister, because she's not her sister. Accept that right now and you'll all be better off. When she sees her star older sister, do you know what she thinks? *There's no way on the planet I can compete with that. She's got "perfect" down pat. That's why I'm going the exact opposite way and making my own path. Maybe then Mom and Dad will notice that I'm me and not her.*

You can't motivate your daughter to do anything she doesn't want to do. What you can do is understand who she is and appreciate the qualities that make her unique. Try these few words for starters: "Honey, I was thinking this morning how many incredible qualities you have."

You've got her attention already. She expected to be hammered for those grades. Instead you're complimenting her? Now she's all ears.

"For starters," you continue, "you have such a kind heart, like when you rescued that abandoned kitten sitting all alone in that cardboard box in the rain. You're always willing to help, like when Mr. Ellis hurt his back and you got his mail and raked his leaves. Those and many other things make you special.

"You're different from your sister, and different is good. Your sister's so perfect, she can be a bit over the top sometimes, huh? Well, I don't expect you to be like her, because you're not her. You're you, and I love you just the way you are."

An opener like that does wonders in taking the sting out of any sibling competition. When kids know their work is appreciated, they'll try harder in everything, even when they don't think they're good at it.

Self-Worth

"I don't understand how it happened," one mom told me, "but my daughter has terrible self-esteem. She's so insecure she can't even go to school. I try to drop her off, but then I have to bring her home with me."

That child was only four, and her mom was talking about pre-school. Of course that child didn't want to go. Children like routine, and this was a shake-up of her rituals. She also was an only child who hadn't socialized with peers, since Mom and Dad both worked long hours and she'd only been in Grandma's care. Why would she be eager to go to a noisy place filled with kids her age running around and an adult or two she didn't know? If I were her, I wouldn't want to go either.

But that has nothing to do with self-esteem. When parents tell me how "insecure" their kids are, they're usually unaware of some key points.

First, insecurity is, at its root, self-focus. If you're insecure, you think everyone in the room is looking specifically at you, so you can't move forward. When you're looking at yourself, you don't see others who may be in the same boat, struggling with the same issue. You don't reach out to others, because every situation is all about you. Every bad thing that happens is aimed directly at you.

Second, self-esteem—what you think of yourself—is overrated, is misunderstood, and keeps lots of shrinks busy. I can't count the

Characteristics of Children with Healthy Self-Images

- They are responsible and capable.
- They are confident of themselves and their roles but not cocky.
- They are sensitive to the needs of others while also taking care of themselves.
- They focus on what they can give instead of what they can take.
- They always try to do their best but aren't hung up on being perfect.

number of times parents have said to me, "Doc, I'm worried that our child will have low self-esteem." Self-esteem is based on how you feel about and respond to situations. It will change based on your mood of the day and perspective of a situation.

But self-worth—realizing you are unique among God Almighty's creations and so is your place in the universe—is very different. Self-worth is lasting. A situation may not work out well, but that doesn't change how you view yourself. That's why, when you fall down, you are able to get back up, dust yourself off, and move forward. Positive character traits, like the ones we're discussing in this chapter, are the building blocks of true self-worth.

Third, a swift antidote to insecurity or arrogance (the other side of the same self-focus coin) is meeting others who are in a worse boat, perhaps one that is filling up fast with water or even resting on the bottom of the lake. When my five kids were at home, they accompanied me not only in taking groceries to families in need but in spending time interacting with and getting to know those individuals. It was one of the many activities we did as a family to instill in our kids that others are important and should be treated as such.

Honesty

Kids can be embarrassingly honest. Take these two real-life situations.

Jenny's four-year-old son accompanied her to her office when his day-care worker was ill. While she was giving instructions to a coworker, he raced up behind her and wiggled his hands into the pockets of her slacks. "Mommy!" he called loud enough for the stars in the universe to hear. "You have extra pillows in your tummy. They're squishy."

Later, after checking out every diet on the planet over her break, she explained to him that sometimes it's better not to say *everything* you're thinking.

Melanie was called in to school for a "consultation" about her six-year-old.

"I'm sorry to hear about your husband," the vice principal told her. "We wanted you to know that the school is here to support you and your daughter at such a difficult time."

Melanie's jaw dropped. "My husband? Uh, what do you mean?"

The vice principal said gently, "We know he's being incarcerated this week. Your daughter told us."

Melanie's shock subsided as the story unfolded. When the first-grade teacher asked what her daddy did, Little Muffin had said, "He goes to jail on Friday."

When Melanie clarified that on Friday evenings her husband was a volunteer prison chaplain, not an inmate, she and the vice principal had a hearty laugh.

With children, honesty can be sticky indeed. What they see and hear they'll say, often at the most inopportune times. If they answer your phone and tell you it's so-and-so, you'd better take the call. Otherwise that child is likely to say, "My mommy doesn't want to talk to you. Goodbye," and hang up. That could do some damage with your adult relations. What kids experience, they say outright, until they're taught to do otherwise. If you and your partner have a disagreement and your child overhears it, you shouldn't be surprised to hear her broadcast that to her friend or teacher.

Honesty is a good character trait, but it needs to be paired with discernment. Thus, if your child "borrows" a friend's toy when he's not looking, you say, "Is that toy yours?" When your child says no, you say, "Then you need to give it back to your friend. He will be sad his toy is missing." You don't wait either. You walk down those apartment stairs or take a drive. Your child gives back that toy in person as soon as possible. You stand behind him and don't intervene. He says he's sorry and hands it back.

If you practice such techniques along the way, when that same boy is 16 and dings the family car, he'll approach you and say, "Dad, I dinged the car. It's my fault. I was going too fast around the corner and misjudged that mailbox." He won't pass the buck. He won't say, "It's all my friends' fault. They were being loud in the car and distracted me." He'll own the truth and be responsible for it.

Honesty starts with the little things. Want your child to be honest? Then *you* need to be honest in all things.

The phone rings, and your child answers it. It's not a person you want to talk to right now. Do you tell your child, "Tell him I'm not at home"? Or do you thank your child, take the call, and keep your response short?

Patience

In the 2007 movie *Evan Almighty*, actor Morgan Freeman spouts some classic lines: "If someone prays for patience, you think God gives them patience? Or does he give them the opportunity to be patient?"[9]

We parents have lots of opportunities to be patient, that's for sure. So do our kids. Problem is, our own impatience sometimes stalls the chance for them to grow some patience.

Nothing good ever comes easy, my mama used to tell me, and the older I get, the more I know she's right. Patience is a critical quality to have in today's instant-oatmeal world. I once watched a college student stand by a microwave and mutter, "Why does this take so long? I've got things to do."

How do you teach your child patience?

First, you don't grant his every wish like a fairy godmother. If your son wants a new computer game and wants to order it online now, parents who value patience as a character quality would say, "Tell me about that game." After he has the opportunity to gush about all the reasons he has to have it, you say, "Wow, that sounds like a game worth waiting for. Well, your birthday is in five months. If you save up your allowance and put in the money Grandpa gives you for your birthday, you will have almost enough. We'll cover the tax and shipping." Often that item your child just had to have will have changed multiple times by his birthday.

Second, you take note of times your child was patient and toss her an encouraging word. "I noticed yesterday you were very patient with your sister. She can be slow getting dressed, and I know you wanted to get out the door to the park faster. But instead of getting upset with her, you put her shoes and coat by the door so she wouldn't take longer to find those. Then you patiently waited. That was most impressive." You squeeze her shoulder. "That helped me a lot this afternoon too."

Third, you encourage patience by showing that taking the long view has its benefits. "I know it isn't easy to wait for that driver's permit since you're younger than your classmates. But that doesn't mean you can't study the rules of the road now, like they're doing. Then when it's your turn, you'll be even more prepared."

Patience is difficult to attain since it's all too easy to get rattled by surprise events, but it's a key character trait for success. If you don't have it, you'll lose your cool, major on short-term thinking, and spontaneously react instead of choosing your response. If you do have it, you'll be able to see any situation with a wider perspective, stay calm, and power on.

Life Balance

Life is a delicate balance of doing things we love that excite us and having to do things we dislike, like unplugging a toilet, or that merely bore us, like taking out the trash and paying bills. Yet all are necessary.

Children who are groomed to expect Disneyland will be sorely disappointed. If life isn't a constant amusement park ride, they'll think it's unfair, they've done something wrong, or others are out to get them. But if they experience a balance between fulfilling their responsibilities, like assigned chores and homework, and having some fun along the way with friends and family, they'll learn to be balanced in their expectations and outlook.

> Children who are groomed to expect Disneyland will be sorely disappointed.

They'll become the kind of workers who give the best to their tasks. They'll head home on time for dinner, embrace their partner, and actively engage with their children. They'll take a jog with a friend early on Saturdays to stay healthy and connected but return home to make animal-shaped pancakes for their kids so their partner can have a well-deserved rest. In that household, love and fun will abound. Those kids will want friends to come over to *their* house rather than go anywhere else for entertainment.

How do you achieve such balance? The formula is easy: B doesn't happen unless A is completed. What does that mean?

Let's say you tell your four kids, "I know tomorrow is a Saturday, your relax day, but this house is in a bit of a mess. We all contributed to that, so all of us are responsible to fix it. I'm asking each of you to not only clean your bedroom but give an hour to cleaning some other area of the house or garage. I don't care when you do it, as long as it's done by 10:00 tomorrow night. We're going to celebrate our hard work on Sunday by getting our favorite Chinese takeout."

On Saturday your firstborn is up at 6:00 a.m. cleaning her room. By the time your second child manages one toe out of bed, your firstborn has the kitchen spotless. She's already back in her room studying calculus since she has plans for the rest of the day.

After a dose of cartoons, your second child, who loves the outdoors, heads for the garage. He opens the door and jams to his favorite tunes while sweeping out the leaves and tackling the spiderwebs in the windows. When friends come by, he loops them in to help. They turn the cleaning session into an impromptu block party and have a blast doing it.

Your third child sleeps through lunch. When he finally gets up, the house is dead silent. Shrugging, he heads off to play baseball at the lot down the block.

Meanwhile, your fourth child has been busy trying to insert herself into her brother's garage party. She loves the spotlight, and the older boys are a lot more exciting than cleaning her room. She did try to clean for about five minutes, but the lure of the nearby music and action were too tantalizing.

You, smart parent, don't do any reminding. Instead you wait and watch. Your firstborn already got her job done. Your creative secondborn found a clever way to get his job done and socialize at the same time.

Then there's your third and fourth children. Your third straggles home at 9:01 p.m. after having dinner at a friend's house and forgetting to let you know. He's tired, so he crashes in front of a movie his dad is watching. At 11:00 he gets up off the couch and goes to bed.

Your fourth made some attempts at cleaning her room, but you can barely tell. It looks like the piles have only been rearranged. She didn't touch anything in the rest of the house.

On Sunday you order Chinese—your and your spouse's favorites, and your firstborn's and secondborn's favorites. It arrives and smells wonderful. All your kids come running.

"Wait." You hold up a hand. "Remember when I said on Friday that I wanted all of you to clean your rooms and spend an hour cleaning the house on Saturday?"

Your older two nod vigorously. Your younger two halt in their steps. The thirdborn frowns, as if only remembering the assignment now. The youngest simply looks confused.

"If you did what I asked, then enjoy your feast," you say. "If not, then you can enjoy whatever else you can make yourself for lunch."

Your two younger kids' jaws drop in shock. They try all kinds of guilt-inducing arguments: "But that's not fair" and "You're so mean." They turn on the tears.

You don't budge from your stance. Four of you enjoy a delicious Chinese feast. The other two look on sadly as they contemplate that jar of peanut butter in the pantry and fight over the last smidgen of jelly and bread in the fridge.

The next time you ask for cleanup, don't you think the response will be different? All your children know you mean what you say and will back it up with action.

Your older two, who did as you asked, received a reward and the satisfaction of seeing those annoying younger siblings get in trouble.

Your third child, who forgot the assignment, now understands the importance of organization and balancing fun and responsibility.

Your baby of the family got a shock. Nobody rescued her or did her work when she allowed herself to be distracted. Next time, she's more likely to start a job and finish it, especially since babies of the family absolutely hate being left out of any party.

That lesson will linger in the back of all four kids' minds in their future choices.

Kindness

Being kind to others isn't natural. Babies come into this world self-seeking and self-focused. They cry when they're hungry, wet, hot, or cold, or have a doodle in their diaper. They bite baby brother or baby sister when they're jealous of Mom spending too much time with the newly arrived mess-maker. That baby of the family will later be the conniving instigator who yells, "Mom! She hit me!" and gets big sister in trouble as her daily entertainment.

Then adolescence hits, and emotions swing wildly. The "it's all about me" thinking peaks painfully when a teenager is surrounded by peers who match that self-focus. Kindness is not the rule of the school jungle. It's eat or be eaten. Waking up with one pimple means becoming the target of "pizza face" remarks and other ridicule. But become the head of the food chain and a kid's own blemishes might be hidden by their big talk . . . at least temporarily.

Kindness may seem like the antithesis to getting ahead in a world of competition, but it's a necessary ingredient of life. Kindness really does make the world go round.

Think of all the successful people you know, the ones who've influenced you the most. Was it because they competed with you or were intensely self-focused? No, likely it's because they were kind, and that trait of kindness led them to do a special action you'll never forget. At your weakest moment, when you needed courage or inspiration, they took time for you. They encouraged you, patted your shoulder, or stood up for you.

How do you teach kindness? You can't tell a child, "Be kind to others." You can only show what that looks like. If another person offends you, do you automatically assume they did it intentionally? Or do you give them the benefit of the doubt by responding kindly and calmly?

Dr. Leman's 10-Second Solutions

Q: I grew up with the "It's all for one and one for all" think-ing in my family. But my own kids' mantra is more like, "It's all for me and me for myself." How can I turn that around and get some help around here? Like even get-ting the kitchen cleaned up?

A: When you're a family, everybody pitches in. Nobody gets off scot-free. You're not the maid or the doormat; you're the parent. Your kids need a wake-up call.

It's time for the bread-and-water treatment. The next time your kids ask you for anything, say, "Sure, you can get/ do that. You'll have to take care of it on your own, though."

"But you always . . . ," they'll complain.

"Yes, I have in the past," you say calmly. "But from now on I'm going to be busy doing things for myself. You can handle whatever you need done."

Snap a mental picture of those confused faces to relish later. Once they realize you're really not going to do those things for them, they'll pull out every tactic in their "How to Work Mom and Dad" playbook. They'll argue, they'll plead. But nothing will work because you're smarter than that.

After a few days, when life is not the same—their fa-vorite shirt isn't washed; dinner is whatever they can find in the pantry or fridge, and that's getting old fast; and no magic genie cleans up after them or finds their lost shoe that the dog dragged under the couch—those kids will be asking a more serious question: "Uh, are you okay? I mean . . ."

That's when you give that answer you've been gleefully fine-tuning in anticipation of this moment: "Oh, me? I'm

> fine. Never better. I just decided that I don't want to be
> the maid around here like I have been. Either we all pitch
> in together to get things done and help each other out,
> or each of us is responsible for our own meals, cleaning,
> laundry, etc."
>
> Let there be light.

If your 11-year-old storms into the house looking like a thundercloud, do you say, "What's wrong with you? Get that look off your face"? Or do you let that thundercloud blow on by? Then, later, you gently say, "Looks like you had a rough day. If you ever want to talk about it, I'm all ears." You don't push. You walk away and let him come to you when he's ready.

If you disagree with your 14-year-old, do you confront her head-on in front of others? Or do you ask to speak with her privately and then engage in a respectful dialogue?

If your child is grieving the end of a first crush or the death of a pet, do you say, "Just get over it. It's been a week. It's time to move on"? Or do you say gently, "I know this has been a difficult time for you. I'll always be here if and when you need me and want to talk"?

Kindness begets kindness. If you major on kindness in your family, minor irritations won't turn into major ones. Let's say one of your teenage girls wears the other's sweater without permission, gets a stain on it, and forgets to wash it. You can be a good role model in showing them how to handle such things without engaging in sibling warfare.

Going head-to-head won't solve the problem. It will likely exacerbate the problem into a tit-for-tat revenge. But suggesting your older daughter say kindly to the younger one, "Oh, by the way, I saw a small stain on my red sweater. If you happened to wear it, I'd appreciate it if you could wash it. Thanks," without any accusing goes a long way toward maintaining family equilibrium.

Kindness starts with you. How you respond makes all the difference in how your children will respond. As an elderly Iowa farmer I know used to say, "Better to err even a little in kindness than to err heaps in the other direction."

Your Turn: Making Your Dream Qualities List Come True

Look back at your dream qualities list from page 29. Taking them one by one, ask yourself these questions:

1. Why did I pick that as an important character trait? Is it because I value that quality, because the lack of it has caused problems with or for my kids, or because of some other reason?
2. What might the end product of that character trait look like in my kids' lives five years from now?
3. What one thing can I say or do this week to encourage that trait in my kids?
4. How could I role-model that trait more effectively for my kids, who are always watching?

Growing the Behavior You Want

Want to know the biggest of all secrets about behavior? *It only continues if it works.*

Yes, you read that right. Those cherubs of yours who come in assorted sizes and packages will only keep doing what they're doing if they are rewarded by getting what they want.

If the "gimme" toddler is pacified by getting the treat she wants at the grocery store, it worked.

If the new kindergartener wraps his leg around Mom and refuses to let go at the school door, guilting Mom into taking him home, it worked.

If the elementary schooler ropes Dad into doing her science project for her, it worked.

If the adolescent who dissed his mom is still allowed to go to his soccer game the next day, it worked.

If the two warring siblings who interrupted their work-at-home dad's business call still get to go to Taco Bell with the family for dinner, it worked.

If the teen who slept in three days in a row is rescued by Mom writing him made-up, "legitimate" excuse notes for being late to school, it worked.

> Want to know the biggest of all secrets about behavior? *It only continues if it works.*

Kids are masters of manipulation. They know how to work a system . . . and how to work you.

But there's a huge benefit to knowing that behavior only continues if it works. You can use that secret to grow the *positive* behavior you want to see. That's because you get what you expect, and they return in kind what they see and hear. If your expectations are reasonable and you win their participation, you'll be amazed at the transformation in your home.

What you expect, you get.

If you expect the worst, you get the worst. Saying to your kids, "If you do X," followed by a threat, doesn't work to control them. It actually primes them to act up. After all, such an act is like catnip to curious kids.

Let's see if Mom [Dad] really means that, they think.

When tired, distracted, or trying-to-be-their-friend parents don't follow through on what they say, that kid smiles. *Aha! I've got their number. I don't have to do that activity I hate. I just have to wait a bit until they're sidetracked, and I can do my own thing. Even if they notice I don't do it, I'm not going to get in trouble . . . at least not for long. They always give in when they ground me. Hey, this is easy, now that I've figured it out.*

If you don't think kids are that clever, go to your local grocery store. Check out the typical interactions between parent and child to see how smoothly this process works for even a three-year-old.

"I want that, Mommy," the little angel says and points to a desired item.

"Not today," Mom says sternly. "We have plenty of treats at home."

"But, Mom, I want that," the child insists and reaches for the item. Mom moves the cart away from the item.

The child whines. "You *always* get me something at the store."

Mom powers the cart, with child in tow, down the aisle. The child, seeing his prize disappearing from view, starts to cry.

"Quiet," Mom says, with an eye on the other customers at the store. "I said I wasn't getting that today."

But about three minutes of constant noise later, the cart somehow magically circles back around to that coveted item. It ends up in the child's possession.

Amazing how well that works, isn't it?

Imagine, though, if that mom would have said before heading out the door to the store, "I'm glad you can go to the grocery store with me. I love it when we do things together. Because you act like a big boy and don't fuss, I can always take you to the store. That makes me very happy."

What happens in that grocery store will likely be a very different scenario.

There's nothing children want more than to make their parents happy. Their favorite audience is you. That's why they put on so many shows with their siblings to grab your attention.

If you raise your kid to think she's the center of the universe, you shouldn't be surprised when she acts like it. But if you rear her to realize she and everyone else on this planet have an equally unique and important role, she will act on that concept in everything she does.

> If you raise your kid to think she's the center of the universe, you shouldn't be surprised when she acts like it.

Great expectations can make a great difference. Try out that concept and see for yourself.

What they see and hear from you, they'll say and do.

People think of sheep as stupid, though sheep lovers and some research scientists would beg to differ. But if you dress up a fake shepherd, sheep won't follow him even if his "voice" is a digital recording of the true shepherd's. Those sheep will gaze at that fake shepherd, listen momentarily, and then ignore him and go back to grazing.

Kids, who lack life experience, are sometimes as stupid as sheep. How else do you explain their tongues getting frozen onto swing-set poles, their shoes stuck in freshly poured sidewalk cement, or chocolate pudding from the lunchroom thrown at a principal's backside when they assume she won't be fast enough to catch them?

But those same kids have an uncanny ability to swiftly spot anything that's fake from yards away. If you ask them to do what you don't do yourself, why should or would they heed your requests?

Thus, for good character traits to become an inherent part of your little and big characters, you must consistently act out those virtues you seek. Lectures and talking about what your kids *should* be like won't get you anywhere. As ol' Ralph Waldo Emerson once said, "Don't *say* things. What you *are* stands over you the while, and thunders so that I cannot hear what you say to the contrary."[10] To colloquialize his wise words: "What you do speaks so loudly that I cannot hear what you say."

The next time you set expectations, make sure you follow them thoroughly yourself.

If you want her to be diligent in finishing her tasks, then finish cleaning out the closet you started on two weeks ago.

If you want him to be thoughtful of others, you be thoughtful. When he has a big test coming up, write a note saying, "You can do it!" Then add a smiley face and tuck it into his backpack as a surprise. When a neighbor's daughter is injured, bring the family a meal.

If you want her to be patient, you be patient. Flying off the handle when any small thing goes wrong won't teach your child to keep anger in check. But a measured counting to five and then the calm words, "Well, *that* isn't what I expected. I'll need to figure out another way to do that," provides a life lesson about balance.

Children are good at mimicry. What you say is likely to come out of their mouths. What you do is a cookie cutter for their behavior.

Your expectations need to be reasonable and voiced reasonably.

At a recent seminar, a midforties couple told me they'd had their son later in life, after they were already entrenched in their careers. They wished he'd get more serious about his goals. When I asked what they meant, they told me he "frittered away" his time after school by not starting homework until after dinner. On the weekends, he wanted to spend time with friends instead of studying an extra language at the Saturday academy they had their eye on.

"He needs to be able to compete for good jobs someday," his dad told me. "That means applying himself now to get the highest grades. If he can keep a 3.8, he'll get into the best high-school academy. Then if he can keep up a second language on the weekends and get a 4.0 there, plus play a sport, he'll be a shoo-in for an Ivy League school."

That kid was only 13, and his parents already had his life planned out. Now is that reasonable? If you were that kid, wouldn't you want to participate a little in choosing your own activities and career someday?

Living the life you wish you'd had through your child isn't fair to that child. Think back a few years. Didn't you hate it when your parents butted in to your business? Then why would you try to control your child's life in that way?

We parents mean well, but in our drive to make our kids top dog, we don't give them the opportunity to try life their way. Sure, they may fail sometimes. Other times they'll succeed. But those failures and successes are *theirs*.

Whether your expectations are heard has everything to do with how you express them. Often we act like Moses at the top of the sacred mountain, collecting and then giving out edicts like they're the 10 Commandments: "Now hear this. . . ."

But if you make such pronouncements, your child's ears will close instantly. Think about it. Do you like it when people make pronouncements about what you should do and tell you how you must do it, without taking your ideas and feelings into consideration?

Neither does your child, no matter how old he is. Just like you, your child is a human being, entitled to his own opinions and dreams.

You need to win their participation.

If you encourage your child's participation on an age-appropriate basis, your expectations will not only be heard but more likely be adhered to.

Let's say you have three children. How could you encourage and win their participation so they come to their own conclusions rather than you lecturing?

Child #1: Your youngest is six. She really wants a puppy and is lobbying hard. You ask her to make a list of what she would need to do to take care of that puppy. When she finishes, you sit down with her and go over the list point by point. You compliment her on her ideas and slowly introduce other concepts, such as, "What do you think we should feed that dog? Where would we get his food? How much would it cost?"

> If you encourage your child's participation on an age-appropriate basis, your expectations will not only be heard but more likely be adhered to.

Have her do more research on how much a puppy of the breed she's interested in eats every week and how much that food costs. She can count how much she has saved and figure out how many weeks or months she'd be able to feed the puppy. Also have her figure out a schedule for when she'd need to walk and feed it.

After she's completed all those steps, say with a smile, "Let's give it a try for a couple of weeks. We can use one of your stuffed animals. Which one would you like to use? You can figure out some pretend food, water and food bowls, and a leash. Set aside in a separate container the money that you'll spend on that dog every day. You're in charge. Why don't you give your dog a name?"

You watch your six-year-old as she goes through the process of caring for that stuffed animal as she would a real dog. When she forgets to feed him in the morning, she comes home to find him lying on his side in front of the empty food dish.

"I guess your doggie doesn't feel very good. He's pretty hungry since he didn't get food this morning," you say.

Note you don't say, "You forgot to feed the dog." You merely point out the oversight.

At the end of those two weeks, you'll have a much wiser six-year-old who realizes taking care of a pet is a lot of work. She's also seen her allowance stash and birthday money disappear fast into that other container.

And you? You've saved yourself a bucketload of cash and aggravation. You won't be doing what most parents end up doing: assuming complete care of the pet their child wanted and soon neglected.

Child #2: Your middle child is 10. He wants to go to camp this summer, but you're on a tight budget. Five days at camp costs $250, and it's only three months away.

You tell your son, "Grandma and Grandpa said they'll pitch in $125. So how much do you still have to raise?"

Your son does the math. "$125."

"Any ideas for getting the money?" you ask.

He brightens. "I know. I can ask Mrs. Jasper if I could pick up sticks in her yard."

You nod. "Good idea."

Your son eagerly races to the neighbor, who agrees to the work. That weekend he picks up sticks all Saturday and comes home with $10. You suggest that he might want to keep a paper tally of how much is left to earn and that he put his money in a safe place.

As he gets new ideas, you listen and bring up other suggestions. You watch your son's motivation in doing any kind of work soar.

A month before camp, he still has $75 dollars to earn, and his weekends have been so busy he hasn't been able to play with his friends. It's not going as well or as fast as he'd hoped. Discouragement has settled in.

You give him a hug. "I see how hard you're working. Earning money is pretty tough, isn't it?"

"Yeah." He sighs.

Every Friday you and your family get takeout. Each of your kids gets to choose once a month, and you choose the remaining Friday. It's his Friday and you know he'll want pizza. But he approaches you and says, "Is it okay if we don't order pizza and use the money it would have cost toward my camp?"

"Sure!" you say. "But all of us still need to eat. Any suggestions?"

Your son makes spaghetti all by himself for the first time. It isn't gourmet, but that slightly overdone spaghetti with canned sauce makes you smile because of the lesson he's learning about cold, hard cash.

A week later, your son comes to you again. "Camp is really expensive. I was thinking maybe my friends and I could make our own camp this summer. We'll play games and do sleepovers at each other's houses. Do you think you could make dinner the night they sleep at our house? The guys and I are going to all pitch in money to buy snacks. You could use the money I earned to make dinner."

You smile. Look at what your son has learned merely because you played along with his dream but didn't provide an easy way out. Now he understands hard work and that money doesn't grow on trees. He came up with his own creative solution for a camp-like atmosphere. It will be a memory he'll never forget because it was his decision.

Child #3: Your oldest child got his driver's license a month ago. He's a good student, very responsible. But for three weekends in a row he's been MIA in the family car. It's time to reel the lad in, since there are places you need to go.

However, you know that drawing up rules about the use of the family car might backfire if he resents you curtailing his newly won freedom. Therefore you say casually, "I was wondering about your plans for the weekend. Since there are five of us in the family who need to go places on the weekends, what do you think would be fair regarding you using the car?"

He swallows hard and thinks. "Uh, what about if I use the car once a month? Would that be okay?"

You lean in to throw a curveball. "To be honest, I was thinking that a couple of times a month would be more fair."

Your son blinks, shocked. This is a better deal than he'd ever imagined.

"It doesn't matter whether it's a Friday night or a Saturday afternoon or evening," you add. "As long as we could arrange it a couple of days in advance so everybody knows, and your mom and I aren't left high and dry without a car for a necessary errand."

"How about if I download a calendar page every month and we all mark when we'd like to use the car?" he suggests.

"Great idea! That would be an easy way for everyone to be in the loop and add their own events."

See how easy it is to win a teenager's participation and favor? You can bet that kid will adhere to the new expectations, especially because he helped set the rules himself.

When we Lemans used that method in our home with our five kids, it worked out well every time.

When you loop kids in and allow them to be part of family decisions, they're much harder on themselves than you'd ever be. And when you win their favor in such a way, you know what they're thinking? *I've got the coolest parents ever.*

With each of your children, you served the tennis ball of life directly where it belonged in those situations—right into their court. Because they were the ones not only participating in but fielding those decisions, they had no room to complain about what wasn't fair. They experienced the steps along the way and the consequences themselves.

Now, isn't that far better than them throwing *you* a curveball? Or you throwing a fastball their direction and hoping they catch it?

A Winning Combo

Cultivate rock-solid character in your kids, and benefits abound. If your children have virtue-driven character traits built into their experience at home, they'll be able to weather any storm they might face as children, adolescents, or adults. Character is the foundation for any transformational change in behavior. The two are integrally intertwined.

If your kids gain the ability to discern, they'll know what to do, when to do it, when not to do it, and how to navigate any situation. When a knuckleheaded peer says, "Bet you could jump off this roof and not get hurt. Jimmy did it off his, and he's fine," your wiser-than-average child will reply, "I don't think so. I know some basic math. Jimmy's house has only one floor. Mine's a two-story. Besides, that's a dumb idea, and my dad told me not to fall for dumb ideas. I'm not a bird, and I can't fly."

> If your kids gain the ability to discern, they'll know what to do, when to do it, when not to do it, and how to navigate any situation.

If your kids are patient, they won't be hopping from foot to foot and getting in your face like a pesky squirrel, saying, "Mom, can we? Can we? Huh? Huh? Huh?" They'll take your no as a no. Of course, if you show any whit of acquiescing, they'll try that tactic again later. They are kids, after all. They've got more willpower and determination than any of us give them credit for. We get tired a whole lot faster. That exhaustion is what kids count on, in fact.

Remember your endgame. When your kids have endurance for the long journey, they'll be able to ride out the topsy-turvy waves of changing body parts. Even when the gossip chain and peer acceptance change as frequently as they change underwear, they won't be dismayed because they know they belong to you and you've got their back.

If they have healthy self-worth, they won't cave when a classmate gives them an opportunity to cheat on a test. Your daughter already knows the rewards of working hard and doing her best. Sure, she might get a B- on that tough test in a subject that's difficult for her, but she knows you stand behind her, celebrating her best efforts. That's far better than getting an A and wondering if others might discover she cheated. Or, worse, thinking she got away with it and trying it again in college or on the job, where the fallout likely will be far worse.

When they have self-control, they won't impulsively do what they'll regret later. Your son won't take advantage of a bully's misfortune, even if that bully deserves it. He'll take the high road with a well-timed, "I'm sorry for your loss," and a straightforward gaze into that bully's eyes before walking away. He won't allow others' actions to control him.

When they have moderation, they won't undereat to look like a model or overeat because they are unhappy and friendless. They won't undersleep or oversleep. They won't underexercise or over-exercise. They'll learn how to handle stress without lashing out at others, hitting walls, or secretly cutting their bodies in areas they think you won't notice.

When they have inner courage and strength, they'll stand as strong as a lion against anyone who tries to take advantage of them. They won't allow themselves to be used or abused. She won't put up with a stalker boyfriend. He won't be drawn into a gang. She won't accept what others think she is but will decide who she is and act accordingly. He won't fear the unknown that looms when he isn't accepted into a college but will forge a new path.

When they have a sense of justice and fairness, they will fight for what is right and stand up for others who face discrimination. He'll say, "Cut it out" when his friends pick on the new kid. She'll hug her best friend's brother with Down syndrome in front of their friends and pull him aside to talk with him. She'll ignore social media gossip and form her own opinions about others.

When they are gentle and humble, they will be the ones who pull up a chair and sit next to a lonely person. He'll bring home that rain-soaked lost puppy. She'll hug her baby brother who flushed her earbuds down the toilet and help him find a lost toy. He'll get the best grade in the class but tell only you. She'll share only good words about her classmates. He'll refuse to play one-upmanship games.

When they have wisdom, they'll be the ones their friends flock to for advice, instead of their often misguided, misinformed peers. She'll be the one you count on never to tell your secrets. He'll stay calm even when under siege.

When they're generous, they'll give of their time and resources to those who have less or are in need emotionally or physically. She'll be the 6-year-old who shares her lunch with the new kid at school who forgot his. He'll be the 17-year-old who stops his car by the side of the road to help change a tire for a stranded single mom with three young kids.

When they have faith, hope, and love, they won't abandon those traits even in difficult circumstances. Yes, they may waver, but they won't cave.

As beloved UCLA coach John Wooden once said, "Be more concerned with your character than with your reputation, because your character is what you really are, while your reputation is merely what others think you are."[11]

When your children live in a virtue-driven home where they naturally assimilate positive, foundational traits, good character will become part of their DNA, so to speak, and good behavior will naturally follow.

STRATEGY #3

GIVE AND YOU SHALL RECEIVE

How respect and a winning attitude powerfully unleash your child's motivation.

I recently visited a class of sixth graders upon a teacher's request to talk about a surprising topic: how much I hated school when I was a kid. To show I was too cool for school in those days, I even modeled my swag walk, shoulders swinging impressively side to side.

"I thought I looked good, but I was just a jerk," I told the kids. "My main goal in life was to be noticed, and I'd do anything to accomplish that."

You see, I had a perfect sister, eight years older, and a nearly perfect brother, five years older. They had a running start on me, the baby of the family, and I could never catch up. Sally and Jack were bursting with good behavior and excellent grades, held top positions in school organizations and teams, and even managed to still be helpful around home.

I couldn't compete, so I did what I could. I decided to carve a different path in life. Jack was captain of the football team, and

Sally was lead cheerleader. Me? I was the school mascot who could run onto the field and entertain during halftime.

When that path proved successful, my mantra of "I have to get people to notice me" became entrenched. I became the school show-off. I got people to pay attention to me because I *made* them pay attention.

It wasn't until much later in life—toward the end of high school—that I realized I had some skills others didn't. That eureka happened because the teacher I mentioned earlier, who had watched me get into hot water many times, pulled me aside and told me I could make something of myself if I tried. Instead of labeling me a troublemaker, she showed me respect as a fellow human who, like all other humans, had some things to figure out about life.

That teacher also had a winning attitude. She believed that even a kid like me could contribute to others' well-being on planet Earth. She urged me to look beyond myself and my constant striving for attention, to identify what my gifts and long-term goals were.

As I look back, that conversation was a significant mile marker, prompting me to get more intentional about my life.

When kids see themselves as worthy of respect and useful, they have no need for negative, self-destructive, or attention-getting patterns.

Why Respect Starts with You, Not Your Child

If you buy or adopt a puppy, do you wait a year to start training? No, for best results you start training right away. Children are more like puppies than you might think. They also need training.

The last time I visited second graders, they were busy talking to each other when I entered the room. I didn't trumpet my presence. I didn't say, "Okay, kids, quiet down. An adult is present." I merely stood until they noticed I was waiting to speak to them.

When a hush descended on the room, I smiled and said, "I'm so proud of you guys. You didn't know I was coming, and it took a little time for you to wind down. But now you're all quiet. I want to thank you for your respect. Now let's have some fun."

In the middle of that fun, some of the children got so excited they started talking over each other. So I established some ground rules. "When one of you talks, I want to listen. That means the rest of you will need to listen too, instead of talking, or I will have a hard time hearing. I will give each of you the same courtesy when you talk to me."

As each child talked, I'd take a step toward them, cup my ear, and lean over to listen. That, parents, is respect. It can't be caught as a concept unless it's not only taught but role-modeled.

Kids are hedonistic by nature. They think about themselves and only themselves unless they are taught to do otherwise. But a onetime attempt won't change things. Kids need to *see* respect in action on a continuing basis. If they don't know what respect is, how can you expect them to give it to you?

Respect is a two-way street. You have to give it to get it. Just because you're the parent and they're the children doesn't mean they will automatically respect you. Fearing consequences for negative actions is not the same as respect.

Parents who say, "You better respect me, young man [young lady]" are barking up the wrong tree. They will never get respect that way.

Respect is not only taught through role-modeling but earned from spending time together. Respect is a *relationship* that's built from your earliest interactions onward. It's one in which you take into consideration the feelings, thoughts, and wishes of others. Yes, you may be quite different from that person, but you see their admirable qualities and appreciate their achievements.

> Respect is a two-way street. You have to give it to get it.

As your children listen to your words and watch your actions, they're busily evaluating these concepts:

- Do you do what you say you'll do? Can he count on you?
- Are you fair and open-minded? Do you hear her side of the story before lambasting her or exacting punishment?
- Do you not only listen to him but actively seek his ideas? Or are you too busy with your own endeavors to take the time?
- Do you allow her to make her own decisions, or do you make them for her? What does that action say about who you think she is and what she's capable of?

Seven Big Don'ts That Parents Do

1. Don't overindulge your kids to buy their affection. Gifts never replace time, attention, and a lavishing of unconditional love.
2. Don't be judgmental; leave that for Judge Judy. Stay out of your kids' business.
3. Don't try to be your children's friend instead of their parent.
4. Don't do for them what they should do for themselves. That tells them they're dumb, incapable, or both.
5. Don't treat them as "less than" you just because they're young.
6. Don't make your older kids parent your younger ones. That's your job.
7. Don't be a know-it-all. That's your teen's job, until he realizes he really doesn't know it all.

Your children's answers to those questions help to shape who they believe you are and who they think they are. They also directly impact your relationship with them, their self-worth, and their potential for success. If you show your children respect, they tend to return it in kind and develop a strong self-worth that fuels them to power through any situation with a healthy balance.

Thus, how you parent has everything to do with your children's success in life. But where did your parenting style come from?

What Type of Parent Did You Have?

Parents tend to fall into one of three basic types, often affected by their background and the type of parenting they were reared with. If there are two parents in the home, each of them may have a different, and often opposite, style. The words parents choose to use reveal their basic type.

When you grew up, which of the three sets of comments below were you most likely to hear from the parent you interacted with the most?

Set #1

- "Eat it. It's good for you."
- "It's time to go to school. No ifs, ands, or buts. We're going."
- "What happened to your backpack? I told you not to lose it."
- "Don't you dare question me. I am your mother [father]."
- "You got a B. A *B*. I expect more from you, young lady. You're not going to make it in life with that kind of half effort."
- "Get back here this instant. You will not treat me that way. And don't you dare slam that door. If you do, you'll be grounded for a month."

- "Kids at school were mean to you? Well, what's your problem? Why didn't you stand up for yourself?"

Set #2

- "Oh, you don't like mac and cheese? I thought you loved it. I'll make you something else."
- "It's okay if you're late to school. I know you've been tired. I'll write you a note and say . . ."
- "You left your backpack out in the rain? Don't worry. We'll go after school today and get you a new one."
- "I'm sorry I made you upset. What can I do to make it up to you? Do you want to get some ice cream? Pizza?"
- "Oh, you got a B in gym! Well, isn't that great? At least you passed one subject. We should celebrate."
- (Your parent follows you down the hallway and stands outside the door you've slammed shut.) "I know you didn't mean to yell at me. You're just upset. Do you want to talk about it? How can I help you?"
- "Who hurt you? What did they do? Do I need to talk to their mother?"

Set #3

- "I know peas aren't your favorite veggie, but they're your brother's, and that was his choice today. Tomorrow is your day to choose. The day after that, it's Dad's."
- "Yes, I see it's already 8:00 and that you'll be late to school. Tomorrow you might want to think about setting your alarm earlier. Shall I give you a ride? You'll need to check in with the office to explain why you're late before you go to class."
- "Sure, you're welcome to get a new backpack. Check and see how much you have left from your allowance, and I'll

take you to get one. You'll need to find one that works with your budget."

- "It's okay and very normal to have different opinions on a subject. That's a good thing, because it leads to interesting discussions. We can all grow smarter by listening to broader perspectives. However, what's not okay is treating each other with disrespect."

- "You got a B! That's fabulous. Congrats. I know chemistry is a hard subject for you to grasp, but all that extra work is paying off. Well, what do you want to do to celebrate? I can't wait for you to tell your mom when she gets home. She's going to be excited for you too."

- "I don't appreciate the tone you took with me this morning. In fact, telling me you hated me hurt my feelings. So I don't feel like taking you to your friend's right now, or anytime tonight."

- "It looks like you had a rough day at school. If you ever want to talk about it, I'm all ears. But if you need time to yourself to work through it, I completely understand. I often need time for processing too before I talk to others."

Perhaps you had a second parent in the home, visited them on weekends or holidays, or gained a stepparent while you were growing up. Which set of the comments above sounded most like them?

Why They Did What They Did and Said What They Said

Remember what I said earlier about behavior, that a child only continues that action if it works? The same is true of parents. They only continue their behavior if it's gaining them something.

Parent #1: "I know what's best, so do what I say."

These parents make decisions *for* their children—they're the parents, after all. They've lived longer, so of course they're smarter. They're most comfortable calling all the shots and announcing how events should go.

If you had such a parent, you were used to living in fear of the consequences of displeasing Dad or Mom. If you dared to question their judgment, you were told, "Do as I say." If you dared to go against one of their dictates, grounding for the next month was the least of your worries.

When you got older, you tended to handle your own problems before your parent found out about them. If you didn't, you knew you might die a social death in front of your peers if your parent showed up to handle the problem for you.

You also stepped gently around them, since they tended to be rather volatile. You weren't allowed to raise your voice, because you were a kid, but that same rule didn't extend to them as the parent.

In public, this parent seemed like "Parent of the Year" because they appeared supportive and always had your back. Behind the scenes, though, you felt you were constantly under pressure. Your grades were never good enough. You were a failure if you didn't make first-chair violin or win the blue ribbon at the track meet. Every day you felt you disappointed them because *you* weren't good enough. You kept reaching for that high bar of perfectionism that was always moved higher, no matter what level you attained.

When they pointed out your failures and lectured you about working harder to succeed since nothing in life is a free lunch, you learned to nod in response until they were done haranguing you. You'd already learned the hard way it was best not to say anything and to simply endure it. But you couldn't wait to get out on your own.

What you did outside of their eagle eye would probably shock them if they knew. But those actions were the only things you could own for yourself, since your parent never allowed you to make any decisions. After all, you were dumb, might fail, and could embarrass them.

Once you moved away from home, you didn't want to go back, except when you were forced to for a dreaded holiday meal. Then you endured your parent telling you why your job wasn't good enough and you should try harder, or giving you specifics about how to be a better parent.

Even though you might now be 40, you know you'll still never be good enough for them. On one hand, you feel the weight of letting them down. On the other, you've built up a thick wall of resentment. On the surface you smile and interact, but all you really want is to get out of there and go home.

Males who are taught from babyhood on that men are the head of the home and that women are subservient tend to be a large percentage of these authoritarian parents. However, women aren't immune to this tendency.

A hairstylist told me that she stopped serving a client of hers because that woman executive would bring in her two children for haircuts and lecture them the entire time—in front of all the other clients—for whatever she thought they'd done wrong that day. The seven-year-old boy was called a "loser with no attention span" for getting out of his chair to investigate a butterfly outside the window. The nine-year-old girl was called a "failure" because she had not won a place in her grade's spelling bee.

A photographer who was shooting for a modeling assignment shared with me that he told the modeling agency he'd barred a mom from a shoot after an unfortunate event. When the beautiful 13-year-old was on lunch break and the event coordinator had provided turkey sandwiches, the mom yanked the food out of her daughter's hand. "Don't eat that. You'll get fat. And if you get fat, you can't take pictures. Then you won't be worth anything."

Dr. Leman's 10-Second Solutions

Q: "No" is my six-year-old's favorite word. Ask him to do anything and that's his response, like it's preprogrammed. How can I change his behavior? It's getting old really fast.

A: Well, his response *is* preprogrammed, and you've done a good job reinforcing that programming. If you don't believe that, let me ask you, what happens when your kid says no? Your blood pressure rises, you become more energetic, and words like these fly out of your mouth: "I'm your *mother*. What I say goes, so you are going to . . ." and "Get your shoes on right now. I'm not going to say it twice." Am I right?

That youngster is baiting you, and you're falling right into the trap. He's got you wrapped around his finger.

Try this instead. The next time he barks no to a request, simply say, "Okay." Then walk away. You'll completely confuse the kid. Kids love ritual, and you've just broken one of his.

Likely he'll run after you. "But you're supposed to say *X*, and then I say *Y*. Get it right!"

You continue to walk away. He may become frantic, but you don't turn around. You get busy doing something else and ignore him. When he wants to do something later, you say no firmly.

"But why can't we?" he whines.

You swivel to face him. "Because I don't appreciate all the times you tell me no. It doesn't feel very good, does it?"

He'll backpedal with all kinds of tactics: "I love you, Mom," "I didn't mean it," "I'm sorry," and one of the worst for moms to handle—turning on the faucet of tears.

Still, you don't cave. You don't do what he asks.

He learns Mom means what she says.

The next time he opens his mouth to spout no, he'll probably think a bit first. If he's hard-core and wants to go a second round, you double down on the same tactics. It's no fun to do what no longer works, so eventually he'll give up.

Authoritarian parents often control their children out of their own fear that their kids won't succeed (the woman executive had fought her way to the top of the ladder by being tough) or that they won't be good enough (the model's mother had always wanted to be a model herself but never made it, despite a couple of years of trying when she was a teenager). Some keep a tight fist on their children because that's the only way they know how to parent.

Parent #2: "Don't worry about it, dear. I'll take care of that for you."

These parents make decisions for their children because they don't want their children to suffer anything uncomfortable or inconvenient. But in doing so, they do the same thing as Parent #1: they rob their child of the ability to make choices and experience the consequences of those choices now rather than later, when the stakes can be much higher.

These are the overinvolved parents who live for their children instead of for themselves. Without their children and their role as mom or dad, they aren't quite sure who they are or what they should do. Thus, every little thing a child says, does, or experiences impacts them directly, like it happened to them.

They're great rescuers. "I know you had a long day at school today. I'll feed the dog and take care of the dishes tonight. We don't need to tell your father about it. You go get some rest."

They're blind to the truth about their child, even when it's in front of their face. "Suzy's not like that. She'd never set up a fake social media account or attack another girl with language like that. There's no way your information is correct." Such blindness makes them insanely loyal, which can be to a child's short-term benefit. But it doesn't help in the long run when the girl Suzy slandered on social media tells her mother, and that mother secures the proof and hires an attorney.

They're experts at manipulating the truth on their child's behalf. "I'm sure Nathan didn't mean to hit that boy. His face must have collided a little with Nathan's fist when he fell. You know, boys scuffle sometimes. It's no big deal."

They're masters at trying to smooth ruffled feathers. "You know she didn't mean what she said. She was just upset. She'll get over it. You forgive her, don't you?"

They snowplow their kid's roads. "Johnny had a stomachache, so he couldn't study for his math test. Can he take the test next week or maybe skip this one?"

They remind their child, "Now, Henry, say thank you to Grandma for that nice present she gave you."

They try very hard to be their child's friend, which can be embarrassing. Especially when that child is an adolescent and his mom decides to cheer him on at his soccer game, wearing a shirt that announces, "Proud to be Justin's mom" and bringing pompoms in his school's colors.

When there are two parents in the home, one is often authoritarian and the other permissive. Any kid who has even 1 percent of a brain will learn how to masterfully play the game of manipulation.

Your son wants a new skateboard. So what does he do? He waits for Authoritarian Dad to get out the door to work and talks Permissive Mom into not only taking him to the store after school but paying for the skateboard out of her grocery fund for the month.

Your daughter wants to go to a concert she knows Authoritarian Mom would hate. So what does she do? When Mom is busy with her brother, she hightails it to Permissive Dad puttering in the backyard. "Dad," she says, "I was thinking I don't get to spend enough time with you. I was wondering if you'll be willing to drive me—oh, and a couple of friends—to a concert tomorrow. I was thinking after we dropped them off later, you and I could get a late-night snack and talk." She reels him in like a fish who has no idea how he got hooked.

Permissive parents may seem like pushovers, but they're actually as highly controlling as authoritarian parents, just in the opposite

Dr. Leman's 10-Second Solutions

Q: My daughter hates math. Whenever I try to help her, she cries or gets mad. She says it's too hard and she's just not good at it. How can I help her get through this?

A: Whose homework is it? It's hers. You already did your time in school. Math may not be her thing, but knowing some basic math is a necessity in life. Trying to "help" her will put a wedge between you that will impact other aspects of your relationship.

It's far better to get an outside tutor who can spend a few hours a week with her after school to give her a different perspective on the pesky subject she hates.

You provide the snacks and the smiles.

direction. To ensure their child's success, they control what she experiences, smoothing out any ripples before they reach her.

Take Keisha, for example. Her parents had her late in life, after their other two were almost out of the nest. She got their full attention, to her detriment. Her can't-we-all-just-get-along mother went out of her way to secretly undo any pronouncements her do-it-my-way-or-else father made. Mama meant well, but her tactics undercut Keisha's ability to navigate difficult people like her father. When a boss got on her case later for not completing a job and she turned to coworkers for help, they didn't back her like Mama always had.

"I'll take care of that for you" parents take away responsibility and the self-worth that doing a job well brings, weaken their child's ability to evaluate options and make good choices, and stall the lessons learned from making poor choices.

Parent #3: "Let natural consequences do the talking."

These parents don't automatically make decisions for their children. They're *authoritative* because they put the ball of authority in the court where it belongs instead of always holding on to it, like an authoritarian or permissive parent would. Sure, when they handed that ball to their child, it sometimes bounced around a little. It even got flung out of bounds. But how can kids learn how to dribble or shoot baskets if they're not allowed to hold the ball?

Authoritative parents not only allow their kids to make age-appropriate decisions but encourage such decision making. Even a toddler can learn lessons about the power of making decisions if a parent starts with the small things and allows the little nipper to experience the consequences.

"You can have a turkey sandwich or a tuna fish sandwich for lunch. Which would you prefer?" Mom asks.

If the child says turkey but changes his mind midway through Mom making the sandwich, she'll say, "Yes, tuna does sound good. But you've already chosen turkey, so we'll go with that for today."

Some of you are thinking, *If I did that, my kid would have a screaming fit and ruin my day.* Well, would you rather ruin one day or every day until your child turns 18, when he'll learn the hard way that others won't put up with his antics?

It's time to nip such behavior in the bud now. An authoritative parent sticks to the decision made. Otherwise the child learns nothing. If he pitches a fit, the parent simply walks away. She leaves that sandwich mess on the counter. When the child realizes his audience has left, he follows and begs, "But I want tuna."

Mom responds calmly, "If you're hungry, you can finish making your turkey sandwich in the kitchen." She doesn't continue making the sandwich. She doesn't give in to his incessant requests for snacks midafternoon. Either that kid will eat a very messy turkey sandwich he makes himself, or his stomach will take over and complete the reasoning process at dinner.

Was Mom mean? No, but she wasn't a pushover either. She merely let the natural consequences of hunger do the lecturing for her. I bet if she asks that child tomorrow what he wants for lunch, he'll think it over a bit more before he opens his mouth to make his selection.

You may not be crazy about painting your son's bedroom walls purple, and you may think a grape-flavored birthday cake is disgusting, but you can still respect that choice as your child's. When his purple phase wanes, simply hand him the white paint and a roller. It will probably take three coats to cover that purple, but he'll get that experience too. And what's wrong with a grape-flavored birthday cake? It'll make for some unique birthday memories and maybe a lifelong love of grape jelly.

As the child grows, authoritative parents loop him or her into the family decision-making process. Want to take a short family vacation this summer? Give your child basic parameters: the range of days and budget you have. Let your budding internet guru do a bunch of research for you and learn about how expensive hotels, meals out, and traveling can be. Then when you do take that vacation, your child will have given input and had a reality check. There will be a lot less whining about the trip, and your entire family time will be more pleasant.

Instead of giving a lecture that will fall on deaf ears, an authoritative parent lets reality do the talking.

Authoritative parents highlight personal responsibility and accountability. Passing the buck of blame or inducing guilt doesn't work with them, nor do they use it themselves. If they make a mistake, they own it, learn from it, and then move on. They know how to say, "I'm sorry" and "Please forgive me."

Instead of giving a lecture that will fall on deaf ears, an authoritative parent lets reality do the talking.

Here's what reality says when it talks:

- Forget to turn your homework in? Then you'll get a bad grade, or the teacher will call you out in front of class while the girl or guy you're crushing on watches.
- Have a fight with your sister? Don't be surprised if she won't drive you to the mall the next day.
- Leave your bike out in the rain? You might need to do a lot of scrubbing to get the rust off the chain.

See how smoothly and easily that works? The authoritative parent knows that the best way to grow positive character qualities is by using and providing experiences that teach those qualities. What kids see is what they do.

Want a child who knows the value of a dollar? Give your five-year-old a buck. Have her go to the grocery store with you and see what that dollar can buy. When you go to the store next, make your list in advance, and have your 11-year-old research what each item will cost.

When your teenager says she needs new clothes, say, "I'll make you a deal. I'll give you 50 bucks toward some clothes if you help me clean out my closet and we clean out yours too." That clean-out will accomplish several missions. First, you'll likely discover never-worn treasures that might displace her and your urge for something new. Second, you'll get organized. Third, when you donate clothes, she might get curious and discover a whole new way of shopping. After all, that $50 will go much farther at a resale shop. My own teenagers discovered thrift shopping and became masterful at it. Even as adults, they're still thrifty shoppers.

Want to teach self-control? Then respond kindly to the neighbor whose cat yowls outside your bedroom window every night. And as delicious as those brownies are, eat only one . . . okay, two . . . and not the whole pan. As they're baking, say to your anticipating children, "Boy, that sure smells good, doesn't it? It's hard to wait. But sometimes waiting makes things taste even better. I'll call you when they're out of the oven, and we can each have one."

I've always said, "The family who works together and plays together stays together." In authoritative homes, the family works together and plays together. Nobody gets off scot-free. Everybody pulls their weight in helping out. If they don't, natural consequences do the teaching.

If your 14-year-old says he doesn't want to clean out the garage, reply, "Okay, that's your choice." Then hire the neighbor kid to do it at the going rate and pay him out of your son's allowance. It works even better if that neighbor is the same age as your son and talks about his windfall at school. Sometimes peer pressure and embarrassment can be a motivating force.

That weekend your son gets a much slimmer allowance envelope with a receipt in it for services rendered. When he's trying to save for a clunker car, money will do the talking.

Parents who are insecure have a high need to control their children's lives by being too prescriptive and demanding or by letting them off the hook too easily. They react to situations with their emotions rather than responding by engaging their brains first. But parents who are comfortable with themselves are more able to see their kids' uniqueness. Instead of insisting they choose a child's path, they encourage that child to pursue his or her own particular bent.

If you're an authoritative parent, you know you're not put on this earth to relive your life through your children or to make them into a "mini-you." Just because you became an accountant but wanted to be a rock star doesn't mean your daughter should become a rock star in your place. Just because a son grows up in a family of chefs doesn't mean he wants to take over the chain of family restaurants.

Just because you're an extrovert doesn't mean your son should be pushed into activities. Perhaps he's an introvert who needs more time to regroup at home from the chaos of school. If you're an introvert, you may struggle with the din when your home is invaded continually by your daughter's social network. But if respect reigns in your family, all of you could agree on at least one "family only" evening each week.

Authoritative parents neither make pronouncements nor excuse their child from consequences. Knowing they are at the top of the hill looking down at life and their child is at the bottom of the hill looking up prompts these parents to offer wisdom but not force it. They set their child up for success by helping her grow character traits that will aid her both now and in the future. But they don't push their child toward success. They accompany her along life's journey as she discovers it for herself, even when that means making mistakes and learning from them.

What Kind of Parent Are You?

Now that you've identified the parenting style or styles you grew up with, skim each set of comments on pages 75–77 again. Which one most closely resembles *your own* parenting style?

Think back over the last few days of interactions with your children.

Have you made pronouncements of what they should and should not do? Have you made decisions for them rather than allowing them to make their own? If so, you tend toward the authoritarian parenting style, where you like to call the shots. It's safer and easier that way.

Do you tend to be a "fixer" for your kids? Do you do their homework or rescue them from consequences? Do you feel bad when they yell at you? If so, you tend toward the permissive parenting style.

If you could identify with the authoritative parent because you already let life lessons do the talking instead of pontificating yourself, then good for you. Maybe *you* should write this book. Then again, if your kids are one and three years old, I'll catch up with you when they're in their midtwenties. I'm sure there will be a lot more fodder for discussion.

Remember back before you had kids and you promised yourself, "I will *never* say or do what my parents did to me if I'm ever in that situation with my kids"? Well, what happened when you got into that situation with your kids a week ago? If you're like many parents, not only did you say what your dad said to you, but you did so at a louder volume. You also did exactly what your mom did, only more dramatically.

You see, we all are impacted by the environment we grew up in. But that doesn't mean we're fatalistically programmed to become a clone of our parents, with no way out.

When you understand why you react the way you do, you can then choose to respond differently. Reacting is a gut impulse that happens without much thought, but it can be trained. When you respond, you ask yourself these things before you open your mouth or act:

Okay, this event happened before.
What did I do last time? Did that work?

Nope. It just got the entire family worked up.

So what will I do differently this time, for a more positive outcome?

If you change your behavior and begin thinking and acting like an authoritative parent—which includes showing respect for your children—then your child's behavior will begin to transform.

Why You Should Never Treat Kids the Same

"I was taught to always keep things equal when it comes to my kids," a man in his thirties told me at a conference. "But even when we do, our kids always fight. What's wrong with them? Or with us? It seems my wife and I can never do anything right."

"What's wrong with them? They're just being kids," I said. "They've found a way to push your buttons. As long as their behavior is working to get your attention, those kids will fight no matter what you do. As for what's wrong with you, you're letting them push your buttons. That means they're winning. And when one side wins, the other side loses. But you're missing a big point. You're trying to keep things equal, when none of your kids are the same."

Take a look at the cubs in your den. None of them are the same, so why should they be treated the same? When parents work hard to view life behind the eyes of their unique children, they'll realize each child will see and experience events differently. They'll seek to understand their kids' personalities and how natural bents lead each child to interpret the same events varying ways (more on this in Strategy #7).

For example, a child who already pushes herself hard to excel doesn't need any additional push. What she does need is affirmation, understanding, and some perspective that being imperfect is not only okay but expected. A child who would never think of the word *study*, especially if the sun is shining and friends with a baseball are around the corner, may need gentle reminders that life isn't all about baseball . . . unless he makes it to the major leagues, that is.

That's why I'm completely against treating kids the same. They are not the same, and you do each child a disservice if you act on that false concept.

Currently you play the role of parent, while your child plays the role of child. However, once that daughter or son of yours leaves the nest, relating to them in an authoritative style is still critical. If you try to tell them what to do, don't acknowledge their adulthood status, or rescue them from poor choices, you do them a disservice.

That's why now is the time to give your child respect and to make some changes in your parenting style. James, a dad I know, loves his two kids tremendously but struggles to connect

> I'm completely against treating kids the same. They are not the same.

with them emotionally since his own father was distant. He never asked his kids what they thought about a situation. Instead he announced what they had to do, then left the room because he was uncomfortable saying anything at all. His children misinterpreted his actions as being cold, standoffish, and disrespectful of their wishes. It was a relational impasse.

But I applaud that dad's courage. After being an authoritarian for 15 years because that was all he knew how to be, James decided he wanted to do parenting differently. He approached his 14-year-old son and said, "Brian, there's something I've wanted to tell you for a long time. I just haven't known how. Honestly, I've been scared to tell you. I want to say I love you. Always have and always will. Saying that is hard for me, because my own dad never said it to me. But I was wrong not to try with you. Will you forgive me and help me do things differently from now on?"

Three Parents Respond to the Same Situation

Your child is having his first day at kindergarten tomorrow. You know he's particular about the clothes he wears. Here's how three types of parents would respond.

Call-the-Shots Parent: "I'll put on the chair the clothes you have to wear to school tomorrow. Make sure you're dressed. Breakfast will be served promptly at 7:30. By 7:45 we'll be in the car."

Smooth-Life's-Roads Parent: "Oh boy, tomorrow is your first day at school. You're going to look so cute in your new clothes I bought for you. I bet everybody there is going to love you and think you're special. Which of all your clothes are you going to wear? What should I make you for breakfast? When do you want to leave for school?"

In both options, your child has already tuned you out. You may like collared shirts, but that doesn't mean he does or that he wants to wear them to kindergarten, unless he absolutely has to. They're scratchy, stiff, and not colors he likes.

In the second option, he already knows you're exaggerating. Not everybody loves him. In fact, he got in a fight yesterday with his best friend. He doesn't feel special either. He knows he's not particularly good at anything, so

Tears sprinkled my cheeks as he told me what happened next. That father and son, whose relationship had resembled the Arctic, hugged each other for the first time the son could remember.

When things your parents have said and done that hurt you sneak into your own speech and actions, you can say three magic phrases to your kids: "I'm sorry. I was wrong. Please forgive me." Then ask them to hold you accountable to show you really do mean it. Don't worry, they will. There's nothing more tantalizing he won't fall for your cooing. And those three questions? Oh, how he hates questions. That deluge of words makes him dizzy. Why bother trying to sort them out? He knows you'll take care of everything yourself anyway.

Put-the-Ball-in-the-Court-Where-It-Belongs Parent: "Tomorrow is your first day of kindergarten. I bet you're excited. You've looked forward to it ever since your sister went to school. Now it's *your* special day. Pick out whatever you want to wear. I'll leave it up to you. Just get dressed and meet me in the kitchen at 7:30. We'll have your favorite for breakfast. Then I'll help you pack all the school supplies, like crayons or whatever else you gathered from the list, into your backpack."

A lot of the problems that concern parents have to do with clothes, hairstyles, food, and friends—all items that will change frequently as kids grow up. Parents who put the ball in their child's court not only allow but encourage their child to make age-appropriate decisions. Mohawks will go in and out of style. So will low-slung pants and bell-bottoms. Friends in tumultuous adolescence are there one minute, gone the next. What's important in the long term is the status of your child's heart and your relationship.

to a kid than having permission to point out a parent's fault to their face, with no negative repercussions.

Let respect reign in your home. It really is a two-way street.

Why a Winning Attitude Wins . . . Every Time

Zig Ziglar once said, "You cannot tailor-make the situations in life, but you can tailor-make the attitudes to fit those situations."[1] That kind of winning attitude starts with you, parent.

What does success mean to you? Is it focused on external things others see, like the house or apartment you live in, the job you have, or the car you drive? Or concrete numbers such as how many vacations you can afford to take or how much money you're able to stash away in a 401(k)? Or whether your child is able to get into the top local preschool, an elite high-school academy, or one of the top 15 universities in the nation?

Or is your idea of success focused on growing character qualities and relationships? Do you smile when you remember a laughing family around the dinner table? The first time you received a dandelion as a "flower" from your generous, sunny baby of the family when she noticed you were sad? When a teacher called you to say your middleborn had used his social networking expertise to raise funds for a classmate diagnosed with leukemia? When your competitive firstborn withdrew from running as class president for the second year to give another student the opportunity to get that credit on his résumé? Do such memories allow you to sleep well at night, knowing you're doing something right on this tumultuous parenting journey?

If you can remember times like that, it shows you're doing many things right. You've been hard at work teaching your child important character qualities such as generosity, kindness, caring for others, and humility. You're already on the road to raising a successful child. You only need some fine-tuning.

Rejection and failure are a natural part of life, but you can treat them as rungs on the ladder to success with the right attitude. How you see yourself, as a result of your parents' style and experiences, has everything to do with your own parenting style. It also has created your life mantra, which informs how you think and act. Once you understand how that mantra impacts you and your parenting, you can use that information to deal positively and proactively with rejection, failure, and adversity of any kind. Then you can teach your kids to do the same.

What's Your Life Mantra?

For a hint about what your mantra is, complete this statement: *I only matter when . . .*

Here are some examples:

- I'm the center of attention.
- Others like me.
- I can serve others.
- I get things done.
- Everybody likes me.
- People respect me.
- I can do things right.
- My achievements are noted.
- People notice me.
- People do what I say.
- I can help everybody get along.
- I can think through all aspects of a project before I do it.
- I meet my own standards and goals.
- I make people laugh.
- I'm in control.

Here's a rundown on four basic types of life mantras.

The Boss: Doing It My Way

If you answered with comments like, "I'm in control," "People respect me," "My achievements are noted," "I get things done," and "People do what I say," you're a person who thrives on being in charge or at the top rung of the ladder. You tend to be decisive, strong-willed, and a commander-in-chief type. You say what you think, and you're a master organizer, self-confident, and independent.

95

If someone wants to get a task done, they give it to you. It'll be done on schedule and expertly because you're an overachiever who dots every *i* and crosses every *t*. You achieve nearly everything you set out to do, but you take it extremely hard if that event doesn't turn out perfectly. Competence and success in others' eyes are extremely important to you.

Problem is, others can find you bossy and insensitive because you always have to rule the roost. You're impatient if others don't jump to carry out your orders. Underneath it all, you fear losing control, whether at work, at home, or in your social life.

When someone crosses you, you may have a difficult time keeping your anger in check. You tend to be unsympathetic toward anyone who's struggling. You have high expectations of others and yourself. You're not known for your warmth or tolerance. That's why you get along best with people pleasers who swiftly do your bidding. You need to be appreciated, respected, and obeyed.

The Perfectionist: Doing It the Right Way

If you answered with comments like, "I meet my own standards and goals," "I can do things right," and "I can think through all aspects of a project before I do it," you're a person who goes a step beyond merely doing things well. You have high standards, want to analyze *how* things should be done before doing them, and are excellent at planning.

You like all your ducks quacking in a row and know what an end product should look like. Long-range goals are your cup of tea. Lowering your ideals is not a possibility. You love alone time and thrive on deep discussions. You're highly creative and sensitive.

Problem is, you obsess so much over details and the planning that you can easily become overwhelmed and negative. You worry about making a mistake. If your high standards aren't met—or worse, no one seems to care about them—you get sad or even depressed.

Generally, you're respectful of others, but you're suspicious of their motives or annoyed if they want to change anything. You take it personally. Deep down, you feel rather insecure. A super-focus on details gives you a razor-sharp memory to hold grudges. Others find you arrogant, picky, pessimistic, and moody. Those who don't take life seriously or are spontaneous instead of planned get on your bad side quickly.

Loyal to the Core: Doing It the Easy Way

If you answered with comments like, "I can help everybody get along," "Others like me," and "I can serve others," you're a patient, loyal person who gets along with nearly anyone. You tolerate a wide variety of people because you don't like to rock the boat.

You're good at solving problems, so people flock to you. You're consistent in helping others, and you don't get upset easily. You are balanced, adaptable, friendly, and very good at listening. If anyone asks you how you are, you say, "Oh, I'm just fine."

You're a born diplomat because you have a calming influence on everyone around you. Everyone loves you because you're compassionate, reliable, and the one who stays until the end of any project . . . even if you are often slower in getting it done.

Problem is, you're allergic to conflict. That means sometimes you waffle at making a decision because you might offend someone. Because you don't want to disappoint people, they sometimes take advantage of your good nature. You spend a lot of your time worrying about keeping the peace and either sidestepping conflicts or playing middleman.

You tend to switch priorities, so you're not good at meeting goals you might set. That makes you look lazy or aimless to others. Because you're calm, others might think you're shy or you lack energy or enthusiasm for a task or life in general.

Party Central: Doing It the Fun Way

If you answered with comments like, "I'm the center of attention," "I make people laugh," "People notice me," and "Everybody likes me," you're someone who loves being the life of the party. You thrive on being in on any action and are always ready for the next event. In fact, you can't stand being left out.

You're the first one to talk to a stranger. You can make a new best friend in 15 minutes flat. Your animated, playful personality and ability to tell stories attract people to you like flies to honey. You can talk others into doing your work when you don't feel like it. They'll even walk away feeling good about themselves because you're flattering and appreciative in your comments.

What's most important to you is being not only noticed but *appreciated*. You take other people accepting you as a given, but you want people to adore you too. Your favorite place to be is in the center of the crowd, with the spotlight on you.

Problem is, you're incredibly disorganized. You lose items like car keys and umbrellas and frustrate others by missing appointments because you forget them or get distracted. Because you're social, if others can't remember your name, you're offended—even if you can't remember theirs.

Your stories are often exaggerated to make them more exciting, so sometimes people don't believe you. Your "Why worry? Just be happy" attitude works a lot of the time, except for when you need to be serious.

And a budget? What's that?

You're allergic to the B-word: boredom. Because you're charming, you tend to get away with everything, even things you shouldn't, including letting others do your work. You expect life to go your way, since it usually does. That optimism crashes swiftly, though, when others take advantage of your naivete and deceive you.

Dr. Leman's 10-Second Solutions

Q: My daughter majors in socializing and minors in every-thing else. Her grades certainly reflect that. But if she can't get her grades up, she won't be able to get into college. How can I make her take life more seriously?

A: Whose life is it? Yours or your daughter's?

The drive to want a child to succeed is deeply rooted in all parents. However, your daughter's idea of success and yours might be very different, especially if you're an introvert and she's an extrovert.

Instead of sighing over her lack of studying—and the evident results—catch her doing good things. Quietly make some notes. Then approach her one-on-one with those positives.

"Lately I've been noticing the things you're really good at. You amaze me," you say. "You're able to juggle a lot si-multaneously. I could never text, talk on the phone, search the web, and do my homework all at the same time. How you manage that is incredible. Just the other day . . ." You go on to tell the story of one of the sweet things you saw her do for a friend who seemed discouraged. "That showed me once again how special and gifted you are. So I was wondering if you had an idea what you'd like to do when you head to college in a couple of years. If you ever want to share any brainstorms with me, I'd love to hear them."

You've opened the door, so she will share . . . eventu-ally. Meanwhile, your gentle prompting will likely get her thinking a bit about next steps.

You know, Dad's right. I'll be a junior next year, and I should be thinking about college. Wow, my grades aren't looking good. Maybe I should actually study for that next test and see what happens.

You didn't waste your breath lecturing. She took care of that for herself. Worked like a charm, didn't it?

How Your Life Mantra Affects Your Parenting Style

If you're a *Boss* who needs to be in charge, staying in control is extremely important to you. On the positive side, you'll be organized, never miss any of your kids' events, and have their attention because you're the clear leader of your family pack. If anyone attempts to mess with your kids, you'll come roaring out of your cave like a Papa Bear to protect them—no doubt about that.

On the negative side, you care intensely what your friends and colleagues think because you're strongly competitive and care about your reputation. If your son embarrasses you in public, he may be at risk of being grounded until he's 21. If your daughter is disrespectful in words or attitude, you'll have a low tolerance for it, and your temper may flare.

If your daughter is a dreamer instead of a planner, doesn't finish projects, and isn't detail oriented, you'll clash quickly and often. If your son focuses on socializing instead of studying and doesn't appear to be serious about life, you'll work extra hard to make him change his ways so he can succeed in life. You can't stand incompetence.

If you're a *Perfectionist*, the organization in your home will be a cut above everybody else's in the neighborhood. On the positive side, every family member will be able to find their shoes, because you've lined them up at the front door in order from smallest to largest. You'll make sure they have a broad variety of experiences—even cultural ones they'll complain about but might secretly like. You'll be the one who looks before the rest of the family leaps. And you'll make sure each of your kids has "space" or alone time to think and reflect.

On the negative side, you expect your kids to have standards as high as you do for yourself. If your son doesn't have a single planning bone in his body, he'll drive you crazy. If your daughter is a social butterfly who floods the house with her noisy groupies, invading the quiet time that you desperately crave every day, you might feel resentful.

If your son doesn't seem to care about your meticulous schedule and is constantly late for family events you've planned, you'll withdraw, feeling underappreciated. If your daughter cleans her room, you'll reclean it or find a corner of her bedsheet untucked, since her definition of *clean* doesn't match yours. Your attention to detail will undercut your child's self-worth gained in undertaking a project and completing it.

If you're *Loyal to the Core*, you'll always be there for your kids—to listen to them, be by their side as they work, and wait for them to return the first time they take the car out on their own. On the positive side, you'll be patient with their stories, problems, and whining. You'll give them the benefit of the doubt when someone tells you about their antics. You're the one who's most apt to say, "Well, I'm sure she didn't mean what she said. You know she's been under a lot of stress lately." You're the family bridge builder.

On the negative side, your drive to help everyone get along makes it easy for your kids to manipulate you. Because you try hard to please others, you overdo it. You "help" your kids with their homework and solve their problems so they won't be uncomfortable. This shortchanges their ability to handle problems for themselves.

Though you're the first one in the family your kids flock to when they need a listening ear, they wish sometimes you'd tell them what you really think. When your kids are young, they think you're cool, because you pay a lot of attention to them and their friends. As they get older, they think you're bland, boring, old-fashioned, and embarrassing. You get too caught up in their sibling fights because they know you're a good audience.

Since avoiding conflict is important to you, you sometimes don't have your kids' backs when they need it most. You can't risk offending others, so you end up looking weak. You accept disrespect because you don't want to rock the boat. Also, since serving others and sacrificing for them is your mantra, you tend to throw your life into taking care of your children and won't take time for your own needs and interests. This can lead you to feel resentful if they don't notice your efforts or say thank you.

If you're *Party Central*, you're the one the kids plan on for fun. On the positive side, your house will be filled with laughter. You take the edge off of sibling rivalry and the typical tiffs that happen as a part of family life. You're a master at crafting memorable moments. You're the first to cheer your kids on at their events. When your daughter is discouraged and needs a pep talk, she'll come to you first. When your son wants to purchase an item the other parent wouldn't approve, he quietly comes to you. If it's for fun, you'll oblige nearly every time.

On the negative side, if you announce spontaneous parties and expect your serious scholar to be there, you may be sorely disappointed. You'll do fine with your social child because both of you are parties waiting to happen . . . at least for a while. However, your need to stay in the limelight may embarrass her eventually, or you may compete head-to-head for attention.

If your child is self-oriented, you aren't likely to be noticed or feel appreciated, much less adored. When your lack of organization leads to you missing important dates and dropping the ball on critical deadlines, like signing permission slips for field trips or paying the internet bill, your "Don't worry, be happy" attitude will grate on your children. You're not their playmate; you're their father or mother.

Developing a Can-Do Attitude

Now that you understand more about how you developed your life mantra and how it affects your parenting style, you can better assess *why* you and your child interact the way you do. Those interactions have everything to do with your child's path to success.

It's easy to fall into the trap of thinking one of these:

- It's gotta be my way or the highway.
- There's only one way to do things—the right way.
- The more I do for them, the more successful they can be.
- I have to be my child's friend first.

When you do so, though, your actions will reflect that life mantra and unwittingly short-circuit your child's success.

There's a better way. You *can* authoritatively stay in the driver's seat, guiding your family's car while developing a pattern of respect and responsibility, where all work together and play together. As you explore your child's unique interests, communication doors will open. They'll help you stay the course as your baby becomes a little girl, an elementary schooler, a middle schooler, and a high schooler, and even when you tearfully wave her out the door to college or a career, wondering how the years could have passed so quickly.

No matter how long you've been in the trenches of parenting, what missteps you've made, how young or old your kids are, whether they are biologically yours, adopted, or stepchildren, you can start on a new path with them today.

Want to project a winning attitude onto your kids and transform your house? Then change what comes out of your mouth first. Even small changes make a very big difference.

The Magic of Counting to 10 before Speaking or Acting

When I was young, I was taught, "Before you open your mouth and say something you'll regret and can't take back, count to 10."

It's still good advice. For those of you who tend to be quick on the trigger with your emotions, you might want to count backwards: *10, 9, 8* . . .

When you're not sure what to say, it's best not to say anything at all until your emotions are under control. If you must say something after your countdown, then try this: "I'm not exactly sure what happened just now, or why it happened. I think it's best for us both to think about it for a few hours. Then we will get together to talk about it."

The Power of Vitamin E

You, parent, have an abundance of a scarce mineral that's worth as much as gold and certainly more than silver. It's vitamin E. But this kind of vitamin E you won't find in your medicine cabinet. It's *encouragement*. If you give your child liberal doses of encouragement, oh, the places she'll go, as our friend Dr. Seuss said.

Projecting a winning attitude starts with a couple of words. You don't have to be a word maestro to use them. You just have to open your mouth and say them.

"Good job."

Since you've mastered those two words quickly, how about a few more?

- "Wow, you've done it."
- "You figured it out all on your own."

- "You amaze me."
- "That was a super job."
- "How thoughtful of you."
- "You made my day. I was dreading coming home and picking up the family room. To my happy surprise, it's Marine Corps spotless. Thank you!"

Such simple words not only make a child's day but open doors that might seem slammed shut.

Catch Them Doing Something Right

Here's a news flash you should never forget: your kids *want* to please you. When Mama and Papa are happy, then everybody is happy. Your kids are like seals at the local zoo, flapping their flippers together, balancing a ball on their nose, and doing all sorts of tricks to please you. If you throw an encouraging fish or two their way, it's amazing what they'll do.

The more positive words you say to your child, the less they'll act up because they already have your attention. The more you solicit their input and opinions in family matters, the less they'll whine or complain about things that happen at home. Why? Because they have a say in making family rules instead of merely receiving almighty pronouncements.

Just a few changes in the words you choose to use with your child will prompt more transformation than you've imagined possible. Your kids won't step on eggshells around you. They won't fight with each other as much. They'll feel free to approach you and talk about anything. They'll ask for your advice. All of you will smile a lot more and bicker a lot less.

If your children are young, they'll grow up in a home of affirming words, learning about responsibility and consequences from the place where it's safest to learn—your nest.

If your children are in elementary school, seeing things done differently at home than at their friends' houses may prompt intriguing discussion over that Friday night pizza.

If your children are in middle school, where they're discovering their own voice, their friend network, and that life isn't always fair, they'll find a mom or dad who listens to them, cares about their interests, gives them leeway for all those hormones that sometimes lead them awry, and holds them accountable for their actions.

And if your kids are in that wonderfully stretching time of life called high school, even if they sometimes think you're from the Jurassic era, they'll talk when they need to and want to and will solicit your opinion because you don't lecture. As they explore next steps, experience a failure or two, celebrate some successes, and begin to fine-tune what they'd like to achieve in life, they'll know you're there with them every step of the way. You don't rescue or force your plans on them. Instead, you allow them to chase their own dreams in their own way.

This week, instead of eagle-eyeing things your kids do wrong, catch them doing something right. Then go ahead—open your mouth and throw them a fish. Once you get used to it, it's not so hard after all.

All the slapping of fins and the other tricks they'll do for you will make your efforts well worth it.

Success Redefined

Success isn't a benchmark that you reach once and then have achieved. Success will mean something different to each of your children, based on their personality, gifts, and beliefs. It's your job as a parent to set your child up for success, not to push them into it or make it happen for them.

If you build the four foundations of character, good behavior, respect, and a winning attitude, you'll increase your child's potential for success in *every area* of adult life.

She'll be the respected mom of the neighborhood. He'll be the businessman with integrity.

She'll be the head of the local food pantry. He'll be the philanthropist who helps to build a children's hospital.

> It's your job as a parent to set your child up for success, not to push them into it or make it happen for them.

She'll be the creative kindergarten teacher who develops a program for children who are deaf. He'll be the construction worker who's known for his hard-work ethic.

All of them will be known for their big hearts, for never giving up under adversity, and for their generosity of time and resources to those who are struggling. What they have in material possessions doesn't hold one flicker of a candle to who they are at their core.

Now *that's* success worth striving for.

STRATEGY #4

ROLE-MODEL A DISCIPLINED LIFE

Why you, and only you, are the hero or heroine your child craves.

If you've used an iPhone recently, you can thank Steve Jobs, founder and CEO of Apple Inc. But there's something not a lot of people know about Jobs. Born in 1955 to an unwed teenager, he was adopted by a working-class family. Obviously he was brilliant and very talented, but what might have happened if that boy had been adopted by people who were wealthy? Is it possible he might not have accomplished as much if he hadn't learned the value of hard work at an early age?

Think about the concept another way. When you fly in an airplane, you like a soft landing, right? But do you want a soft takeoff?

I don't. I want that plane to lift off the ground in a hurry and hightail it up safely into those blue skies. A plane can only take off well from a hard runway. If the plane starts out on a soft surface, it'll never get off the ground.

When you discipline your child the right way, you start him off on his journey with life success in mind. Yes, the runway may be hard at times, but that hard surface will get him off the ground faster. Living a disciplined life will also allow him to enjoy the ride along the way. Even when a few bumps come, he won't be easily discouraged.

Such success starts with you. Though there's no such thing as a perfect parent or a perfect child, you're the best role model your child has for what a successful life looks like. You may not think so, but she is always watching you and listening to what you say.

> You're the best role model your child has for what a successful life looks like.

Do *you* live a disciplined life? Do your speech and actions match your priorities?

If you say your kids are important to you, do you show up at your son's soccer game even if it means staying up past midnight to finish your work project? Or do you finish the work project earlier, knowing your kid will understand if you don't make it? Or do you pay partial attention to that game by taking your laptop with you and doing work on the sidelines? How present are you with your kids?

If you tell your daughter that money isn't everything and that other things in life are far more important, like spending time together, do you show up at the family dinner table every night instead of taking that promotion that will mean working late many nights? Or do you take that promotion, because then you'll have more money for another car, her sixteenth birthday, a vacation, or college tuition?

Do you mean what you say and say what you mean? Or do you let your temper and impatience get the best of you?

If you've told your young kids not to dress up Rosie the dog because she doesn't like it, but they do it anyway, do you let them off the hook by saying, "They're just kids playing dress-up. I guess the dog has to get used to it"? Or do you stand by your original request? "I asked you not to dress up the dog. Since you decided to do it anyway, I guess Rosie and I are the two who get to go for ice cream this afternoon. You two will be staying home with Grandma." Then you clue Grandma in not to give your two rascals any treats, as much as they beg.

Do you finish tasks (even those you dread) or put them off? If you hate cleaning, and the dust bunnies and hairballs from your cat are about to take over your house, you don't have a good foothold to "encourage" your son to clean his room, which would require a hazmat suit. If you hate checking your bank balance and paying bills, and you put that off until bill collectors call you, is it fair to fault your child for not finishing her math homework?

Do you do the right thing, even when it's hard? Like admitting to your perfectionist spouse you're the dumb bunny who tore the mirror off the car when you misjudged the fast-food drive-up window? Or apologizing to your sobbing daughter because you forgot to show up at her second-grade career day?

All of us need role models who can show us how to live successfully. However, your child already has an ultimate hero or heroine in mind—you. Here's why you, and only you, can make all the difference.

What Your Actions Say to Your Child

The reason I had you look carefully at your parents' parenting styles, your own resulting parenting style, and how that informs your actions is because how you do life models for your child how they should do life. Your actions speak lessons to your child that you might not intend.

The Authoritarian Parent

If you're an authoritarian who has to call the shots, you're unwittingly telling your child three things.

First, *success is being in control.* If your son can't be the one telling others what to do and ordering people around, then he's basically worthless.

Ouch. Not what you intended, huh?

Not every child has the personality and skills to be able to or want to call the shots. Every child marches to the beat of her own drum and should be allowed to follow her own tune—whether it's hard-driving rock, a gentle lullaby, a meandering ballad, or a playful, lighthearted melody.

Second, *you have to be top dog, no matter what it takes.* If your child isn't the top dog his peers respect, look up to, and—let's be honest here—fear a little, then he's nothing. He'll always

Dr. Leman's 10-Second Solutions

Q: When I asked my kid what he wanted to be when he grew up, he just said "Alive" and went back to web surfing. How can I talk about anything with a kid like that?

A: Kids, like husbands, hate questions. Especially if they're intently in the middle of web surfing, even though it may look like they're doing nothing.

The best way to open a conversation is to sit down next to that kid. "Looks like you found something interesting. If you ever want to share anything with me, say the word."

He may not bite the first time, but wait. Continue to show your interest without pushing. "Tell me more about that" is a great opening phrase too.

When you choose to dip a toe into his interests instead of trying to drag him unwillingly into a conversation he doesn't want to have and that suits your agenda, you'll be surprised what you learn about him and his world.

be the low rung on the ladder of life. Competition is everything. Compassion and working as a team are for losers.

Is that really how you want to define success for your child? If so, you're setting him up for a world full of hurt, failure, and discouragement.

There's only one CEO of a company, but that doesn't mean the other workers are worthless. Each part played is integral to having a company in good working order.

What's most important is each child finding her own unique place to happily and passionately contribute her skills.

Those whose parents insist their child stand on a pedestal for all the world to see take a lot of risks that she might be knocked right off on a windy day. A bit of competition can be motivating. But continual forced competition raises the bar so high that no kid can jump over it. No matter what she does, she knows she will never be good enough for Dad or Mom. She will always feel like she's a disappointment to you. Depending on her personality, one of three results is likely to happen.

> *Result #1:* She'll try to power through and meet your expectations, gaining some trophies, good grades, lines on her résumé—and an ulcer along the way, among other physical ailments.

> Ever wonder why an A student would be tempted to cheat on an exam? Devin can tell you.

> "I only wanted to keep my dad happy. It's important to him that I keep high grades. He wants me to get into college on a scholarship."

> Devin got an A in that class he wasn't good at . . . at least temporarily. Three weeks later he and two other test takers who shared that cheating scheme were caught and expelled from their private academy. *That* definitely didn't make Dad happy.

It's even worse if the competitive, calling-the-shots parent decides to do the cheating for the child, with or without their knowledge. Consider the 2019 college admissions scandal, where Hollywood celebrities, college admissions administrators, and coaches were caught doctoring tests, inventing facts like children being on sports teams, and bribing their kids' way into prestigious schools.[1] Those children were betrayed by the ones they trusted most to believe in them. By acting as they did, the parents were saying, "I don't think you can do this by yourself. It's important you get into the right schools, or you'll be a loser. You need our help to get in. If we have to cheat to get you into those competitive schools, so be it." The fallout those children have faced already, and will face in the future, is saddening, sickening, and unfathomable.

That whole sordid mess is a cautionary tale for controlling parents everywhere. If your kids can't get into their favored college on their own, they belong somewhere else. And don't insist on any particular college. You already had your go-round. Now it's time for theirs.

Your child's life is not *your* chance for a do-over. It's *their time* to shine in their own way.

> Your child's life is not *your* chance for a do-over. It's *their time* to shine in their own way.

Result #2: She'll meet those parental expectations on the surface but rebel underneath. What she does on her own time, out of your sight, you probably don't want to know about.

I watched this happen right under my nose at the grocery store. After a mom lectured her eight-year-old, "I told you. When we're at a store, I expect you to behave. If not, there will be consequences," he said blandly, "I got it, Mom."

113

As their cart started to turn the corner, that boy halted for a minute and I saw his face. He mouthed her lecture right back to her sarcastically, then punched his fist in her direction as he proceeded to follow her.

When she turned back and said, "Aren't you coming?" that kid said serenely, "Of course, Mom."

Fast forward a few years to when that kid's in middle school with plenty of peer influence, and what do you think he'll be doing behind Mama's back . . . to the delight of his peers? What about when he holds the family car keys and has more autonomy?

These are the kids whose parents show up in my counseling office, wringing their hands and saying, "What did we ever do wrong?"

Result #3: She'll cave under that pressure and become submissive not only to you but to anyone else who is calling the shots.

That's a recipe for disaster in a world where not everyone is looking out for her best welfare. She'll try and fail, try and fail again, and after a while she'll give up trying and do the bare minimum to get by. She'll give her homework a lick and a holler. She won't stand up for herself when she gets picked on at school. After all, since she's not good enough and she can't do anything right—like even making her bed perfectly enough for you—why try anymore?

All she wants to do is skate under the radar, stay out from under the parental eagle eye, and get out of Dodge as soon as possible. But even then she'll struggle with low self-worth, won't think she's good enough for anyone, and feel she can't do anything right.

Perfectionism is slow suicide for any child because of the high stress it means, day in and day out. Pushing your child to be perfect won't make her more successful. It will harm her in myriad ways.

Critical-eyed parents often tell their kids, "You better make me proud." That simple phrase carries a load of negative weight. It's more like a command: "You better not let me down or embarrass me in any way or you'll pay for it the rest of your life." Parents who do that are revealing their own insecurities. Every child will do something dumb sometimes. It's a fact of life.

Those living under parents who nitpick will often procrastinate in getting things done because they're afraid if that project is evaluated, it won't be good enough.

His dad's criticism worsens how he already feels about himself. He criticizes himself mercilessly for even the tiniest mistake and never forgets when he's dropped the ball. That makes it difficult for him to head into new situations with healthy self-worth.

She feels she can never measure up to her perfect mom. Even when a teacher tells her, "Great job," she thinks that teacher is only being nice.

His self-confidence is a big zero. Even if he happens to stumble into a great accounting job and he's good at it, he's always waiting to be exposed as a failure . . . because that's exactly what his dad said he was.

Kids who live under authoritarian pressure *will* rebel in some way. They might go out of their way to be rude, argue with their siblings, or pick fights at school. Or they'll wait until their college years and combat almost any authority, which doesn't work out well for them with teachers or school administrators, not to mention internship and job searches. Others will become quiet and cooperative on the outside and timid on the inside—unable to risk trying anything new for fear of failing or disappointing you.

If you're an authoritarian parent calling the shots, the third thing you're telling your kid is, *you're too dumb to decide anything for yourself.* If you constantly tell your child what to do, how to do it, and when to do it, you're saying, "You're so dumb that I don't believe you can make good decisions. I'm going to have to do it for you to get this done right."

Problem is, to become responsible, your child has to have the opportunity to *be* responsible. Do things for your child that she should do for herself and she'll learn, well, nothing. Without the ability to make age-appropriate decisions—and even to make the wrong ones at times—your child won't develop the ability to make wise decisions. She'll lack the ability to think independently or to be flexible.

> To become responsible, your child has to have the opportunity to *be* responsible.

Nobody likes the consequences of poor choices. But those natural consequences are the best teacher any child could have. When the results sting a little, he's not as likely to act like that again. Isn't it better for that child you love to experience consequences in your comfortable home, before he's pushed out of the nest to flap his wings in the wider world?

As hard as it is to let go of that control and lighten up on the rules, now is the time to allow your children to make age-appropriate decisions.

You may not like that miniskirt your 15-year-old wears, but if you live in Chicago, the Windy City (and yes, I know "windy" originally referred to Chicago politics and not Mother Nature), and there's an especially windy day, she might rethink that decision herself and at least put leggings under it.

You may not like the way your four-year-old puts away his toys when you ask him to, but let him have his own method of management.

You may shake your head over your son choosing to spend his allowance on buying pizza for all the guys after school, especially if saving money is important to you. But that son will learn his lesson when he realizes he doesn't have gas money for his car the next week.

Allow them their choices and those kids will learn far more about how to live successfully than if you open your mouth and say, "You need to . . ." or "You should . . ."

The Permissive Parent

If you're a permissive parent who likes to smooth the bumps out of your child's road, your actions are saying four things to your child.

First, *success is when you're the center around which everyone else revolves.* Permissive parenting creates what I call "SBS"—Spoiled Brat Syndrome. These are the mini princes or mini princesses who get away with anything and reign over your house because they can. Change their routine and you'll hear about it for hours. They can't adjust because they're used to being the center around which everything at home revolves.

The loud ones are easy to pick out because your eardrums are ringing from their vociferous antics. You do their bidding merely to quiet them down so they don't embarrass you in front of your friends or neighbors. Or maybe because you'd like a little peace of mind and mouth at the dinner table.

But don't be fooled. The "shy" or "quiet" ones can be just as manipulative with their guilt-inducing tactics. If they don't get what they want, they turn on the waterworks. They know it works every time, especially to make a pleaser mama do their bidding. A papa can be easily coerced, too, by a daughter's pleading or tear-streaked eyes.

Children who grow up under permissive parenting tend to be extremely self-centered. Because they're used to getting things their own way, they don't develop empathy for others' situations, much less consideration or generosity. They haven't learned how to care about others—except for what they can get from them—so they can come off as socially inept.

Because they always assume they're number one, they do whatever it takes to stay in that position. Relationships don't last long, because others can't count on them and find them judgmental or critical. Young adult and adult children of permissive parents tend to have at least one area in their lives where they show little or no restraint, such as overeating, drinking, gambling, or one-night stands.

Therefore, if you rear your child to think that no one else but him counts, you're doing him and yourself a huge disservice. Such a concept may work temporarily while he's still young, until his self-centeredness starts to drive you crazy or puts a wedge between you and your spouse, who also wants and deserves some of your time.

And what happens when another critter called a sibling shows up and needs some of Mom and Dad's attention too? Or when your child walks into a room of other children who've also been reared with this parenting style? There will likely be a few explosions, and those in charge of that group of kids will tell you that your child needs to learn how to pitch in with work, help others, and share toys.

No one but God Almighty deserves to be the center of the universe. The sooner your children learn that, the better for them, for you, and for everyone else they come in contact with.

The next time your prince starts his dog-and-pony show for your attention or your princess crooks her little finger, don't fall for it. If you're doing an activity, don't stop. It won't kill them to be told, "I understand you want that right now. But Mommy is busy. I am doing something for your brother. Tomorrow is his special day to bring cupcakes to school. That means your request for me to play with you has to wait. If you'd like, you could help me decorate some of the leftover cupcakes for our family treat after dinner tonight. Otherwise you need to find something else to do."

Then you get back to work on those cupcakes. No whining, no complaining, and no "You just don't love me" and "It's not fair!" statements deter you from your project. Even better if you put earbuds in, listen to your favorite relaxing tunes, and block that prince or princess out.

Second, permissive parents communicate to their kids that *you're not capable, so I need to fix things for you.* This concept has a remarkable similarity to the authoritarian parent. That's because both authoritarian and permissive parents are controlling in their own way. The authoritarian calls the shots for his child because he needs to be in charge. The permissive parent calls the shots because she wants to remove any obstacle that might harm her child.

But if you do things for your kid that he should do for himself, you're treating him as incapable of doing those things. Permissive parents are masters of excuses.

- "I only did that for you because I knew you were tired and needed some sleep."
- "I didn't want you to worry, so I made that phone call and handled it."
- "You have better things to do than gas up the car. I took care of it."
- "Oh, you don't need to do that. You have plenty of other things to do. I'll do it."
- "I knew your science fair project was coming up and you haven't had time to work on it. I did some research and started on one for you. You just need to put a few of the plastic trees on your Dinosaur Island and you can call it done."

Long story short, the parent has done the child's work for him.

To feel true accomplishment and achievement, a child needs to do the work for himself. He needs to experience the highs and lows—the satisfaction of a project turning out well or the frustration of an experiment that doesn't work. He needs to figure out how to innovate when events don't go as planned. Such work teaches endurance and flexibility and improves self-worth. If he can't learn how to solve problems at home, where else will he learn that key skill?

You shortchange your child by handling his work or problems for him.

You shortchange your child by handling his work or problems for him.

Third, *I don't want you to be inconvenienced, stressed, or uncomfortable in any way.* Let me ask you: Are you ever inconvenienced or stressed? Then why shouldn't your child be? Are you always comfortable? Then why should your child be? Life is not Easy Street, where people all do your bidding when you want and how you want. Trying to provide a child with that type of experience produces a child who can't handle conflict, changing circumstances, or anything that doesn't go his way.

If you've paved the way for your child on Easy Street, now's the time to stop. Every person needs to accept that real life happens. It's inconvenient, messy, and sometimes downright aggravating. If your child is constantly bubble-wrapped by Mama or Papa, she won't feel the effects for now. But when she goes out into a larger world, she'll experience the shock of the century, sans bubble wrap.

It's far better to allow your child to experience events and their consequences. Being uncomfortable is what prompts change. A child who is uncomfortable learns patience, tolerance, humility, and a boatload of other foundational character qualities.

The next time your child has her history paper due, don't rescue her. If it doesn't get done, it doesn't get done. If it's late, it's late. If she pitches a fit, yells, and says, "Why aren't you helping me? You always do. What's your problem?" say calmly, "Hmm. Seems like the problem is yours, since it's your paper. Good luck with that. I'll see you in the morning." And off you go, for a much longer night of sleep than you normally would have had so you're out of firing range.

The next morning you don't comment on the dark circles under her eyes or her crabby personality. You don't return her barbs. You simply say, "I'll see you tonight," and wave her off with a smile at the bus as she leaves for school.

Let her experience the consequences of her own work, or lack thereof. The embarrassment in front of her peers or teacher won't kill her, but it may make her think about getting that next paper done on time.

Changing up your child's routine by throwing her a curveball isn't such a bad thing after all. The sun doesn't rise and set on her existence. Lessons learned in light of that reality now will lead to greater potential for life success later.

Fourth, *look at me. I'm a martyr who sacrifices my life for you.* If you're a doormat whose only purpose in life is to keep your child happy, you'll fail even before you start. No child can be happy 24/7. It's not possible, as much as you might try. It also doesn't lead to success down the road in school, career, or relationships. In fact, it does the opposite. It causes your child great harm.

A parent acting like a martyr prompts a child to treat others—especially those of the same gender as the permissive parent—as doormats. No one respects a doormat. It's treated not as a person but as a thing that gets walked on or tromped on and is only good for cleaning mud off of shoes.

Boys who have permissive, submissive moms often look for and marry permissive, submissive wives . . . and the trend continues into future generations. They tend to struggle with female bosses who don't bend to their wishes, who tell them what to do, and who don't let them off the hook for jobs they drop the ball on.

Girls who have permissive dads often look for and marry permissive men they can control. That works for a while, until that wife discovers her husband can't make decisions because he doesn't want to offend anyone. Then she begins to think of him as weak and ineffectual, instead of the charismatic guy she fell in love with who is helpful to everyone, and loses her respect for him.

Don't set yourself up to be used and abused by your kids. You don't deserve that, and neither do they. Taking time out for yourself is not selfish. Rather, it role-models for your child a disciplined life, where everyone's needs in the family are important, where everyone at school is equal, and where all at work are colleagues who play differing roles, banding together to accomplish a common mission.

Don't shortchange your child out of your own need to be needed. No one can grow strong and determined if they are raised to be weak.

The Authoritative Parent

If you're an authoritative parent, if you balance staying in the parental driver's seat on critical issues while allowing your child age-appropriate choices and some autonomy, your actions are saying five things to your child.

First, *I believe you are capable and competent*. The power of belief in your child can't be overrated. Read any interview of a successful person and they will say something like this: "I'm where I am today because someone believed in me."

If your three-year-old is learning how to tie her shoes, she'll learn how to tie them a lot faster if Mom or Dad believes she can do it, gives her some tips about making loops around bunny ears, and then cheers her on.

If your 13-year-old is a budding fashionista and gets the idea of reinventing clothes from a thrift store to wear to school, why not back her? It'll help out your budget and support her creativity.

Dr. Leman's 10-Second Solutions

Q: How much is too much to give a kid? My husband and I grew up poor, worked hard, and now have a more comfortable life. But nothing we give our son seems like enough. He always wants more and makes us feel like we're failing as parents if we can't provide it. How much is enough? Too much?

A: Parents often overcompensate if they've come from underprivileged circumstances. But giving kids things won't instantly make them grateful. In today's gimme culture, kids who have it all will never be satisfied.

You're already giving your son three square meals a day, a roof over his head, clothes, and a good education—way more than many children in the world have. The fact you're providing anything more makes him incredibly fortunate as a human being.

It's time for the gimme attitude to stop. Your son needs a healthy dose of gratefulness, humility, community service, and learning the value of a buck.

Look at opportunities nearby. Make your next family activity a trip to help out at the local food kitchen or a homeless shelter. Give no forewarning. Just pack up the family and go. Even better if you make it around dinnertime, when stomachs are growling. Facing a hunger pang or two will make the experience more realistic.

Cook a meal for an elderly person who doesn't get many visitors, and sit and eat it with them. Shovel a walk for a disadvantaged neighbor.

Your entitled son won't like these a bit. Then again, do you always like everything you have to do? He needs to learn as swiftly as possible that the universe does not revolve around him and his comfort.

Put the cash you'd use for his allowance that week in an envelope. Have him go grocery shopping with you, buy items for families who have hit hard times, and distribute those items. Keep the receipts. That week, when he gets his allowance envelope, put the receipts in there instead of his usual cash.

Again, there's no forewarning, no threats, no lectures. Yes, he'll be shocked and upset. After all, he thinks it's *his* money that you spent without his permission. But that kid wouldn't have any of his possessions without you, would he?

When he finally calms down and asks why, you shoot it to him straight. "Lately we've noticed that you want more and more. We've been giving you more and more. That's our fault. We grew up poor and wanted better for you. But better for you is realizing that not everybody has what you have. Take Ms. Townsend, who . . ." You go on to talk about the people he's met recently and their stories.

When your son interacts with others who have far less, realizes his allowance could feed three hungry families that week, and returns to your palatial mansion with a flat-screen TV and a full refrigerator at his disposal, guilt will likely set in.

Guilt, when used for the right reasons, is a powerful motivator for change. No lecture is needed, only a "step into others' shoes" kind of experience. Let reality do the talking and you'll both be better off.

When she gets the sewing bug, dust off that old machine of your mother's that has been in the basement for years. If she decides to collect scraps of fabric from your neighbors to make simple shirts for a welfare institution in Haiti, tell her, "What a great idea. I love that you're taking this on as a challenge and using your creativity to do something good for people who are struggling. That shows your generous heart."

Children can fly high when you believe in them. Just ask me. Without Mama Leman, who never gave up believing in me, I wouldn't be where I am today. I would not have married my beautiful and capable wife. I wouldn't have five kids I believe in and who believe in me. And I wouldn't have received the precious privilege of becoming a grandfather.

Second, authoritative parents communicate to their kids that *I have no doubt you can and will make good choices*. Authoritative parents don't simply wait for choices to come along for their children. They create decision-making opportunities. They look for what I call "teachable moments"—situations that provide natural consequences and do the lecturing so the parents don't have to.

Lessons are much longer lasting when you let reality do the talking instead of you. Many kids get Mommy-deaf or Daddy-deaf. They tune out whenever they catch a hint of a lecture starting. That "uh-huh" is only a jab at pretend listening. However, when real-life consequences smack them in the face, that can't be ignored. Even better, you didn't have to get in the middle of it.

Passing the buck of blame doesn't work when a decision is solely your child's, and the consequences are also hers.

For example, your fourth grader insists she wants to be in summer soccer. You know that once she realizes it's a lot of running and kicking for practice and then more time standing on the field doing nothing, she'll want to quit within a week. However, her friends are signing up for it, and she's very social. You only have enough money to cover one summer activity.

You say to her, "We pay for one activity each summer. If you choose to do soccer, that will be your one activity instead of camp, like you did last summer."

Initially she's excited, because she's getting what she wants that minute. But soccer pans out exactly like you predicted. She tells you she wants to quit.

You shrug. "Well, that's up to you. It's your activity."

"So I can quit?" she asks, thinking all of this is working out well for her. She gets to ditch boring physical activity.

"Sure, if that's what you want."

She quits soccer, then says she wants to go to summer camp.

Your response: "If you can raise the money you need before camp, as well as the transportation costs to get there—I think gas for the car would cost about $50—you're welcome to go."

Recognition dawns. "Wait . . . I always go to camp."

"Yes, that's true. But this year you chose to do soccer." And you turn your back and walk away.

Your fourth grader misses out on activities for the summer. Since she already quit soccer, the coach—whom you tipped off about the necessity for a life lesson—says he can't take her back on the team. She ends up meandering her way to the outskirts of the soccer field that summer, watching her friends play.

She likely won't be very happy, but she has learned a valuable lesson she won't forget anytime soon. It will make her wiser in her choices at a young age.

My guess is that sometime down the road, when she's got kids of her own, she'll be telling that story to develop some of those traits on *her* dream qualities list.

Third, *I will always treat you with respect because you are deserving of respect.* Children who grow up with authoritative parenting know they have inherent self-worth, because their parents treat them that way. A child can't learn what respect is without first being given it. Respect for himself and others is a critical

Checklist for Being a Positive Role Model

- Do what you say.
- Love unconditionally.
- Separate the sin from the sinner.
- Say "I love you."
- Tell your child what you appreciate about her.
- Admit when you're wrong.
- Say the magic words, "I'm sorry. Please forgive me."
- Model what you want your child to be.

foundation for life success that allows him to expand his processing abilities for new experiences, discover his gifts, and interact in a healthy way with others.

Authoritative parents give kids what they'd want themselves: the benefit of the doubt before being proven guilty. Just ask Brody, who's now 27 but vividly remembers an incident that happened in his home when he was four.

Their family had a pet goldfish, Seymour, that had been part of the clan ever since Brody was a baby. One day while his mom and older sister were mixing up green frosting for a cake, Brody decided to add a few drops—well, quite a few—of that green food dye to Seymour's fishbowl.

Needless to say, that goldfish turned a little green in the gills and soon thereafter kicked the bucket.

When his mom saw the green water and death throes of the flopping fish, she knew exactly who the experimenter was. But she didn't do the typical parent thing. She didn't yell in his general direction, "Brody, you get in here right this instant and explain . . ." Instead she went and sat by him. "I see you added some green to Seymour's water. Tell me about that."

He plunged in excitedly and explained why. It was St. Paddy's Day, and the O'Sullivan family always made a big deal about it. The entire family dressed up in green and had green food. Little Brody wanted their beloved Seymour to be able to join the party. He had no idea the pretty-colored water would lead to the pet's early demise.

Brody will never forget the way his mom approached that situation. He says that remembering it teaches him to be patient with his kids, who are two and four years old, and not to assume the worst before they explain their perspective on the event.

If your kids do something you don't agree with or understand, you might want to ask them about it before jumping to conclusions.

Your nine-year-old son takes apart the toaster. An authoritative parent doesn't say, "What got into you to do that to the toaster? Don't you know we need that for breakfast? What's wrong with you?" Instead, when you wake up to toaster parts all over the table, you say, "Mmm, looks like you've got a project going there. Want to tell me more about that?"

> **If your kids do something you don't agree with or understand, you might want to ask them about it before jumping to conclusions.**

Even though you don't get your usual toast for breakfast, you find out that your son is interested in engineering. He merely wanted to know how the toaster worked. He claims he can put it back together. You're dubious, since you didn't grow up with any handyman bones in your body.

But, wonder of wonders, five days later you have a toaster. It's even calibrated to no longer burn your toast. See how much better that was than yelling? In the long haul, five days without toast was worth it. Now your son is 17 and has been accepted at MIT . . . all because you allowed him to work with that toaster and other electronics in your household.

Fourth, authoritative parents show their kids that *I consider you a unique individual with your own gifts and don't expect a clone of myself.* Authoritative parents look out for their kids' welfare, but they don't live their lives for them. Just because you're a teacher doesn't mean you should expect your child to be interested in education. You may love skiing, but your daughter would rather be a weight lifter. You love to give parties, but your son is more of a hunker-down-in-his-room person.

Differences aren't wrong, they're just . . . different. Once you accept that truth, you can get along admirably with even the child who is the most unlike you. You'll be able to identify their gifts more easily, see those gifts in action, and support them by saying, "Wow! Great job. I can see you've put a lot of time and attention into doing that. It has to feel good to have that turn out well."

Fifth, *life won't always be easy, but we're going to do it together.* Kids who are reared with authoritative parents have a deep sense of security. They know you will be there for them no matter what happens. Home is a place of safety where rules don't change. Family members respect each other and listen to each other, establishing a pattern that anything is fair game for discussion. That keeps conversation flowing even when peers become an important part of your children's lives. When there is support at home, kids can relax. They don't have to compete for affection.

> Differences aren't wrong, they're just . . . different. Once you accept that truth, you can get along admirably with even the child who is the most unlike you.

You also don't expect your kids to be top dog. Instead, you pay attention to what they are interested in and actively work to enter that world. Your kids do the same for you. Because you're family, you're "all for one and one for all"—a team of two, three, four, or more standing together united against any problem.

Your "Transform Day"

Do you really want to rear a successful child? Then decide today that you no longer will be a prisoner of your parents' parenting style. Now *you* are the parent. It's your choice how you will parent.

Make today your "Transform Day."

Find a quiet place. Identify the type of parent you have been, due to your own parenting and other experiences. Acknowledge the mistakes you've made as a result. (Don't worry. You're the only one who's hearing your self-talk.) Then say aloud, "But all that is in the past. I'm not a child anymore. I'm not under my parents' authority. Today I'm going to choose to do things differently. To think differently. To act differently."

What happened in the past prompted you to get to the place you were before you opened the pages of this book. But whether or not that past influences your future is completely up to you. The past only has the power you give it. Today's the day you change your internal dialogue.

Throw away any preconceived notions about parenting that make you feel overwhelmed or inadequate. Leave behind any mistakes you've made. Choose to move forward today as an authoritative parent. Be the kind of parent who becomes the voice in your child's head that says, "I believe in you. I know you can do it. I'm proud of you and who you are"—a voice that will still be heard years down the road.

You see, *you* are the hero or heroine your child seeks and wants to look up to the most. None of the Marvel Comics superheroes have anything on you.

But they do make for some killer storytelling.

STRATEGY #5

DISCIPLINE, DON'T PUNISH

Why reality discipline rocks, punishment ruins, and the three Cs rule every time.

I used to have a cocker spaniel whose name was Trouble. Well, it wasn't really, but it might as well have been.

No matter how much we tried to train her, she wouldn't listen. She had a mind of her own that wouldn't be thwarted. One time she even grabbed my wife's gourmet meat loaf right off the dinner table in front of us and ran off down the hallway with it. Spam out of a can wasn't a very tasty culinary replacement for that meat loaf.

When we told her no, she'd sometimes acquiesce until we were focused on something else. Then she'd slink, catlike, toward that "no" object and make it her own.

We learned our lesson the hard way about making sure we were consistent with our pets. If you don't discipline your cocker spaniel, guess what is going to happen? You'll have a dog that does bad things, like chewing carpet and stealing shoes, and drives you a bit crazy.

Children have similarities to dogs when it comes to discipline. Without discipline, and the consistency and stability it provides in a loving relationship, kids will run awry.

Your Unprecedented Opportunity

Think back a few or a lot of years to when you decided, "Let's have a kid," or it happened unexpectedly. Or to when your dream of adopting a child came true. Did you know exactly what you'd be getting into?

Most of you are laughing at that question, and rightfully so.

If you're like many parents, you might have assumed, "We have a BMW. Maybe we should get a child. You know, one of those little two-legged things that runs around and makes noise. Why not get on the track of Pampers, Pull-Ups, and all those colorful toys for a while? It can't be that hard, right? After all, there's so many of them running around the planet. I bet it would be fun."

Then you got the kid and experienced 2:00 a.m. feedings, colic crying jags, scraped knees, and more. You worked full-time, so you wondered, *What am I going to do with the baby when my maternity leave is over?*

Some of you had Grandma or Grandpa nearby, who agreed to watch the baby part-time for you. You might have been able to rearrange work hours, work some from home, go to part-time, or make other arrangements, like swapping babysitting hours with another working parent. Others of you hired a nanny or found a day-care situation you were comfortable with.

No matter what situation you chose or are choosing right now, I encourage you to remember a critical concept. In the early years, children are wet cement, to quote the title of Anne Ortlund's classic book.[1] The impressions you make on your child's heart, values, attitudes, and actions from the time they enter your home onward harden as they grow older.

That means if you have young children, you have an unprecedented opportunity to change the type of imprint you're making on them out of the gate. Others of you will have to work a bit harder since the cement has started to harden. Patterns will be more difficult to alter. However, no matter their age, you have the chance *now* to make an impact no one else can because you're their parent. They have lots of friends, but only you have such an esteemed title.

That's why you should never easily give up your authority to anyone else. That includes teachers, day-care workers, coaches, after-school program directors, or kiddie kennels of any kind.

The word *authority* these days gets a bad rap. People don't like to use it. They chafe against it. But it's actually a good and necessary word.

I'm no scientist, but even I can understand what a physicist friend once explained to me. The earth's axis is tilted at an angle of 23.5 degrees as it orbits around the sun. Because of that tilt, and the fact that the sun shines on different latitudes at different angles, North America has the seasons of spring, summer, fall, and winter. We also have day and night, in contrast to chilly places in the arctic circle that have 24 hours of darkness in the winter and 24 hours of sunlight in the summer. Over thousands of years, the earth wobbles very slowly, slightly adjusting that angle. However, if the earth would tilt just a degree one way, we'd burn to death. One degree the other way and we'd freeze to death.

Even within creation there are authority and built-in rules that keep all of us as safe as possible on this planet. In the same way, authority in parenting is good and necessary, when used with discernment. You and your child are equal in worth as human beings, but you play differing roles. Your child hasn't been around the block as long. Thus, there are times when, to keep him safe from a world that isn't always kind or focused on his best interests, you have to pull a parental authority card and play it wisely.

The majority of the time, though, you need to keep that ace in your pocket. Allowing your child to make decisions, experience the consequences, and then pick up and move on sets her up for success. It builds confidence, self-worth, courage, tenacity, endurance, honesty, the ability to apologize, and a host of other character qualities that will help her fly in the area of her interest.

Discipline has to be a part of any loving relationship. And just like parenting, discipline isn't a nine-to-five job or a task you pick up after work, like your dry cleaning. It's a 24/7 on-call gig. But

Dr. Leman's 10-Second Solutions

Q: Our four kids fight over the littlest things. How can I get it to stop? Aren't siblings supposed to love and look out for each other?

A: Easy peasy. Stop playing Judge Judy and exit stage left. As soon as your kids realize they no longer have the main audience they want to play to—you—the fight will fizzle. They'll probably look at each other with a bit of embarrassment and then slink away. After all, that whole fight was staged for *your* benefit, to get *your* attention. Your kids are a lot smarter than you think.

They also love and look out for each other more than you might think. They may fight like crazy at home, but at school or in the neighborhood, it's 99 percent likely they'll have each other's backs.

I once saw a third-grade girl body-slam a fifth-grade boy much bigger than her against a school locker because he kept picking on her smaller-than-average fifth-grade brother. Those two siblings were known for fighting like cats and dogs. But there was no way she was going to let somebody outside the clan beat on her brother without doing something about it.

Twenty years later, those two still have each other's backs. Your kids will too.

it's the most rewarding job you will ever have, because it forges a lifetime relationship that gives your child the best foundation for success.

Discipline or Punishment?

When I asked a group of parents what they thought *discipline* was, one father shot his hand up and blurted out, "Getting the kid to do what he's supposed to do."

Nearly everyone in the room laughed. Heads nodded in agreement.

"Fair enough," I said. "That is a goal of discipline. But what happens when he *doesn't* do what he's supposed to do? What do you do then?"

Every parent on the planet knows that a few kids are likely to do what you ask them to do. Some need a bit of nudging. Others are like wild horses that fight any potential for leadership.

If you want to rear a child who will become a successful adult, discipline is a critical foundation in encouraging the development of the key character traits you dreamed of in Strategy #1. Many confuse discipline with punishment, though, or use the terms interchangeably. However, their purpose and process are quite different.

Discipline is the consistent, day-to-day, hour-to-hour grooming of a child to explore, understand, and accept specific values, ideals, thinking, and actions. The goal is not control but learning. It is an intentional process of developing winning attitudes and excellent character that directly impacts behavior. It's not something a parent trips or falls into. It is a measured response, carefully thought out in advance, to preparing a child for the many situations he'll be faced with or currently is facing.

Thus, when specific situations come up, the parent already has a road map for how to handle them. When carried out with love and balance, discipline sets a child up for lifelong personal, relational, and career success.

Punishment is a reaction to a specific circumstance. Reactions are based on the emotion of the moment rather than being a pre-planned response to a behavior. Actions kick in before rational thinking. Often bribes and threats ensue. When neither technique works, punishment kicks in.

To understand the differences between discipline and punishment, consider the following two case studies.

Case Study #1: The Prized Olson Heirloom

The Olson family has a prized stained-glass lamp that sits on their living room table. It is an heirloom crafted by Ms. Olson's grandfather and has special meaning to her.

The Punishment Method

Four-year-old Nathan touches the stained-glass lamp he's been told not to touch. It's a "family heirloom" and "off-limits," his mom says.

He has no clue what that means. He only knows that his mom, who is fussy about other things, is uptight about him touching the lamp.

Bribery stage: "I'll give you a cookie if you leave it alone," Mom says.

He nods, and she gives him the cookie, which he promptly chows down on.

But an hour later the way the sunlight plays on the colors in the lamp is irresistible. Nathan touches the lamp again.

Threat stage: Eagle-eyed Mom spots his infraction from the doorway and sweeps into the room. "Nathan, I told you not to touch that. Your great-grandpa made it. It's not a toy. If you touch it one more time, I'll send you to your room."

Five minutes pass. Mom is nowhere in sight. Nathan heads straight for that lamp and grabs at the red jewel that dangles from it. But this time the lamp falls over, skitters off the table, and crashes onto the floor in a spray of multicolored glass. Nathan stares in awe.

Punishment by the avenging archangel: Mom rushes in, assesses the damage, and blows her cork. "I *told you* not to touch that. Why did you touch it? You're bad. Why are you so bad? Why do I have a son like you? What did I do to deserve this? Go to your room right now. No dinner for you tonight." She points an imperious finger toward his room.

Cowed, Nathan heads off to his room. But his mom isn't done.

The second jab: "And just so you know, we're having grilled cheese sandwiches and tomato soup tonight. Your favorite. And *you* aren't getting any."

Mom turns on her heel and stomps off to the kitchen in a cloud of steam.

The immediate fallout: Punishment is given with highly charged emotion at the moment of greatest impact. Mom, who lost her prized heirloom lamp, isn't rational. All she can see through her red-colored lenses are those multicolored glass shards across the floor. What comes out of her mouth is a gut reaction.

She wants that kid to pay. He's going to get what's coming to him and then some. She's angry he didn't listen—multiple times—to what she said. Worse, he didn't care that the lamp was important to her and broke it. Her entire day is ruined.

Meanwhile, Nathan is hiding in a corner of his room behind his stash of stuffed animals. He knows Mom is angry, but he didn't mean to break the lamp. He merely thought it was pretty and wanted to explore it. His mom often told him not to do things but then let him get away with it. He's confused about why this time is different.

I know, he thinks. *I'll just wait it out. She'll get over it. She'll let me have some dinner when she cools off. I really love grilled cheese and tomato soup.*

But as he sits there, hunched into a ball, he remembers her words: "You're bad. Why are you so bad? Why do I have a son like you?" They hurt.

The secondary fallout: Half an hour later, Mom has calmed down in the kitchen. Those deep-breathing exercises have come in handy. As she starts to make dinner, she feels bad about the whole situation. Nathan's generally a good kid, but sometimes his curiosity causes trouble. Why did she react so over the top?

Guilt sets in especially when she remembers she told him *he* was bad. What kind of terrible mother is she to say that? Much less withhold food from her 42-pound kid?

When it's dinnertime, she slides a tray of food in front of his closed bedroom door. It has steaming-hot tomato soup with a pat of butter and a grilled cheese cut in triangles—just the way Nathan likes it.

"Nathan," she cajoles, "Mommy didn't mean it. I was just mad. I'm sorry. I made you your favorite. Open the door."

When he opens the door, he has a bountiful feast spread in front of him to cover those hunger pangs. Even more, Mom doesn't mention that broken lamp.

But what has Nathan learned? That if he waits long enough, she'll cool down and he won't get punished. So why not touch whatever he wants to? There are no long-term consequences. Mom might talk big in the moment, but she won't follow through, at least not for long.

Fast-forward a few years. Do you think that boy, now a teenager, will treat his mom with respect if scenes like that continue to play out between them?

The Discipline Method

What if this had happened instead?

Mom sees Nathan staring at that lamp. Knowing her ever-curious and exploratory son, she sits beside him. "It's pretty, isn't it?"

He nods. "Yeah."

"I was always fascinated by that lamp when I was little too," Mom says. "In fact, there was one time where I tried to touch the lamp and got in trouble. I didn't think it was a big deal, until my dad explained why the lamp was important."

She tells Nathan about a boy who saved up every penny he could when he was young to buy pieces of glass because he wanted to build a lamp. It took him seven years to create that lamp. That boy was Nathan's great-grandpa.

"That lamp tells a very exciting story," Mom says. "If you are patient, believe in your dreams, and work hard, you too can make things that are unique and beautiful." She hugs Nathan. "Just like your great-grandpa made this lamp."

Before she gets up to return to her work, she says, "If you ever want to touch the lamp, let me know. We can do that together. You have to touch it very, very gently, since it's old."

That scenario took a total of five minutes, but that smart mom created a teachable moment that will last far longer. She used her son's natural urge to touch beautiful things to share a childhood story that wove in character traits she wanted to grow in him: patience, self-confidence, self-worth, the ability to think big, and the passion to work hard.

The final twist? Instead of cutting off her son's explorer trait, she tempered it by saying he could touch the item, but she had to be there when he did.

You see, children don't rebel against things they've been told to do. They rebel against things they're told not to do. Remove that and there's no rebellion. If you expect the best or explain why something is important, you'll likely get the best out of your child.

> Children don't rebel against things they've been told to do. They rebel against things they're told not to do. Remove that and there's no rebellion.

Also, what many parents assume is rebellion is simply curiosity and a lack of restraint. For example, an 18-month-old finds the holes in the light socket in the wall. He tries to stick his finger in. You tell him no, but he does it again. He is looking for cause and effect.

What happens when I stick my pinkie in that hole? Oh, I see, Mom comes running, swoops me up, and does this little dance. It's really entertaining. Let's do it again.

The more parents react and overreact, the more likely it is for that specific behavior to recur.

As for the boy fascinated with the stained-glass lamp, who knows? Maybe he will end up being an artist in his own right someday. He might even create furniture with pieces of colored glass to honor his great-grandpa.

My own son, Kevin Leman II, used to make excuses to skip school sometimes to watch game shows because he found them fascinating. Little did we know that, a couple of decades down the road, he'd be creating his own game shows and become a multiple Emmy Award winner.

So, parent, keep the big picture in mind. Knowing your child and his interests will help you evaluate how to approach any situation in a way that's a long-term win for both of you.

Case Study #2: The Rosaros' Dilemma

The Rosaro family is known for their hard-work ethic and strong family values. Their firstborn daughter, Sofia, recently got her driver's license and her first job after school at a convenience store.

The Punishment Method

Sofia asks her dad if she can take the family car out after school since she has to work later hours than usual, and she wants to meet friends for a bit. Dad agrees but tells her she has to be home by 8:00 p.m. since he and Mom have a community meeting to go to.

Bribery stage: Dad knows Sofia has a tendency to socialize and forget the time. He tells her, "Look, if you make sure to get home by eight, I'll give you $20 to spend however you want."

Threat stage: Before Dad hands over the keys, he adds, "If you're not home by eight, your mom and I won't make the community meeting on time. You know how important those meetings are to us. We'll be embarrassed in front of the whole neighborhood if we're late. So, young lady, you'd better be home when I say, or it's going to be a long time before you get the car again."

"I get it, Dad," Sofia says. "I'll be home."

But 8:00 rolls around and Sofia isn't home. She isn't answering her cell either. Then 9:00 comes and goes, and her parents miss their meeting. They call Sofia's work, and the convenience store says she didn't show.

Sofia arrives home with the car a few minutes before 10:00.

Punishment by the avenging archangel: Dad is waiting for her in the living room. "Where have you been?" he barks out. "Do you know what time it is? Almost 10:00. Your mother and I missed our meeting because of you. I told you to be home before 8:00. Did I not tell you that?"

He doesn't wait for her to answer but plunges on. "I know you heard me. What do you have to say for yourself?"

"Dad, I'm so sorry," Sofia says. "I know what time it is. I know you guys missed your meeting. But—"

He cuts her off. "That's it. I can't trust you with the car. It'll be a long time before we let you have it again. You might even be in college. Now go to your room. Right now."

"But, Dad—"

The second jab: "Just for arguing with me, you're grounded. For a month. I'm going to call that convenience store and tell them I won't allow you to work there anymore. I thought you were old enough to be responsible, but I guess not."

She tries again. "Would you let me explain—"

"No excuses," he states. "You blew it. You can't explain your way out of this."

The immediate fallout: Sofia drops the keys on the living room table and flees to her room. *Dad is always like this*, she thinks, frustrated. *He never listens. And even if he knew what really happened, I doubt he'd care. All he cares about is getting his precious car home on time and going to that meeting. That's more important than his daughter. I am so done here. I can't wait to move out.*

Dad sits in the living room, glowering. He can't believe his daughter was so irresponsible. He thought he raised her better than that. She'd even skipped work, after going on and on about how important making money was to her. But she let him down. Worse, he couldn't trust her to be where she said she was going to be.

The secondary fallout: Sofia spends the next three days avoiding her dad, as hard as that is when she's grounded. She's embarrassed that he called the convenience store and frustrated because she worked hard to get that job. She's given up on him listening to anything she has to say.

Dad's embarrassed too. The day after he yelled at Sofia, his furious wife set him straight. Sofia had gone to her with the real tale of what happened that night. He doesn't know what to do to fix it. Why did he let his temper get out of control? And why hadn't he even asked her why she was late without blowing his top? Now his daughter isn't talking to him and likely won't be anytime soon.

In this situation, what did the daughter learn? Dad couldn't be trusted to hear her out, so why should she talk to him about anything? If she went to him with any problems in the future, he would probably embarrass her, like he did when he called the store and told them she was quitting her job. Most of all, he had no respect for her as a person, much less as his daughter. He'd called her irresponsible and grounded her for helping out a friend.

The divide between them will grow unless Dad learns how to say, "I'm sorry. I blew it. I didn't listen to your explanation when I should have. Please forgive me."

You, parent, are the adult. You should be the first one to step up to the plate to say when you're wrong. The words "I'm sorry. I was wrong. Please forgive me" are the first steps to breaking down any barriers.

> The words "I'm sorry. I was wrong. Please forgive me" are the first steps to breaking down any barriers.

The Discipline Method

Let's replay that same situation using the discipline method.

When Sofia asks her dad if she can take the family car out, he says, "Of course. I trust you. Your mom and I need to leave for a meeting at 8:00, and we'll need the car."

"Got it, Dad," Sofia says.

But she doesn't come home until right before 10:00.

Dad is waiting in the living room when she walks in. She's always been a good girl and responsible, so he knows there has to be a reason why she's late. Still, he can't help but be worried. He hasn't been able to reach her via her cell phone.

"I'm glad you're home," Dad says. "I was getting worried."

"Dad!" Sofia races into his arms for a hug. "I'm so sorry. I know you and Mom missed your meeting. I feel really bad about that. I lost track of time."

He doesn't ask questions. He doesn't say, "And where were you, young lady?" He waits for her to tell the story.

"I had the craziest night," she begins. "Is Mom around too? I want you both to know what happened."

Sofia had been on her way to work when her best friend called, saying her mom was really sick. Sofia drove both of them to the ER, and the mom had been admitted with a kidney stone. Sofia had tried to call work to let them know why she'd be late, but her cell phone had died mid-call.

In the flurry at the hospital, she'd sat beside her tearful friend who was worried about her mom. In the chaos, she didn't notice the time until it was after 9:30. Then she'd hightailed it home.

No doubt that father was glad he hadn't spouted off to his daughter about her being irresponsible with the car or coming home on time. Instead, by hearing her side of the story before judging her, he kept the emphasis of the event on growing their relationship and turning it into a teachable moment.

Sofia, for her part, apologizes for being late and worrying them. "I understand if you don't want me to take the car for a while. I said I'd be home at 8:00, and I broke that promise."

There is the responsible, trustworthy daughter her father knows. She's willing to accept the consequences for helping her friend out.

He waves her off. "I'd say you had a very good reason for being late. We can let this one go. But in the future . . ."

She laughs. "I know. I learned a big lesson tonight."

"And that lesson is . . . ," he prompts.

"That I better pack a charger in my purse and keep it there. Okay with you if I take the extra one that's in the kitchen?"

He smiles. "Sure. That's a great solution."

That father treated his daughter with respect. He didn't blow his top during a stressful situation. He didn't throw out punishments, like grounding for a month, because she was late. He relied on what he knew about his daughter—that she had good character, was responsible, and likely had a good explanation for her belatedness. In short, he had trust in her.

That, parent, is what it's like when you set your goal to rear a successful child. Yes, life happens, and not all turns out like you expect. But the foundation of trust and respect in your home allows both of you to forge a path ahead through any situation while growing your relationship.

Why Discipline Rocks

Everyone makes mistakes. Everyone has flaws. That includes you and your child. Punishment exacted out of anger or revenge won't grow your child's character. Neither will allowing her to disrespect you or continue unhelpful behavior that will harm her personal, work, and career prospects.

Telling a child what to do can work when he's young. Restraining him physically when he gets angry and throws a tantrum can work too. But what happens when that toddler becomes a 100-pound middle schooler or a 190-pound high-school freshman linebacker? Never allow disrespect of any kind to rule your home.

A daughter who has you wrapped around her little finger may seem "cute" when she's young. But what about when she's 13, and she manipulates you to take her places so she can secretly date a boy who's graduating from high school?

What if your son wants you to fill out his college applications because he's too lazy to do them? Are you going to move into that dorm with him, go to classes for him, write his papers, and take his tests too, so he can continue the easy life he's accustomed to?

The two case studies above highlight important differences between punishment and discipline. Punishment focuses on the specific event and categorizes the child as "bad" because of the event. Heat-of-the-moment decisions induce guilt, and guilt never leads to balanced behavior. Overdo it on the punishment and you'll end up attempting to pacify or buy your child off because of that aftereffect guilt. Even though a bit of sweet revenge might feel good in the short term, it doesn't pay or work in the long term. It serves to divide you from your child.

Discipline focuses on the end goal of attaining a desired character quality and developing a long-term relationship. It requires forethought and planning in deciding how you'll act when events occur.

Dr. Leman's 10-Second Solutions

Q: My eight-year-old daughter picks on other kids. This is the third time I've had to leave work after a call from her teacher. Even though I ground her for a week every time, she only shrugs and asks if we're going to get her favorite fast food on the way home. Why won't she stop?

A: Why should she stop? By bullying another kid, she gets four rewards—ditching school, controlling you by making you leave work, getting her favorite takeout for lunch, and having more hangout time to do whatever she wants. Not to mention the rush she feels at being a temporary top dog—before the teacher and principal get ahold of her.

To stop the behavior, you have to stop rewarding it. The next time it happens—and it likely will, if the pattern holds—talk turkey with the teacher or principal. Say you want the bullying to stop, for everyone's benefit. Ask them to hold your daughter for a couple of hours, past lunchtime, without providing lunch. Take your sweet time in getting to the school, after your work meetings are over. Even better if it's the end of your workday.

On the way home, you pass that drive-through.

"You missed it." She points.

"We're not getting food today," you say. Your car doesn't go anywhere but home.

Once home, you don't lecture. You don't ask her what happened. You don't make her lunch. She scrounges for herself.

As she's ready to take a bite, you hand over some papers. "Since you missed your classes today, your teachers gave you extra homework. You also need to write a story for English and present it in front of class tomorrow. I'll see you in the morning." You exit off to complete your work and then have a blissful night's sleep.

What happens or doesn't happen with that homework is her call, not yours. Even bullies don't like to be embarrassed in front of their peers.

If you want a behavior to stop, stop rewarding it. Allow real consequences to do the talking for you.

If you punish your child, you are out of control. You're allowing the situation to direct your feelings and actions and labeling the child because of that behavior.

If you discipline your child, you are in control. You act in your child's best interests to better shape his character. You take the time needed to assess the situation before you open your mouth or act. That time allows you to think through your parental agenda: *What does my child need to learn in this situation to help prepare him for life?* Then you can respond in a way that fulfills that goal.

Lessons from "The Three Little Pigs"

In the well-known fable of "The Three Little Pigs," three pigs each build a house to protect them against a Big Bad Wolf who wants to eat them. Here's my take on what really happened.

Pig #1 isn't all that into work. He only wants to get the job done so he can go about his merry way of doing whatever he wants to do. He wants to give this task a lick and a holler, as a friend of mine used to say. After all, Mama sent him out into the world to seek his fortune, and that's what he's gonna do as fast as he can.

147

He doesn't want to be stopped by any low-level task like putting a roof over his head.

Straw, he thinks. *That would be easy and quick to use. Besides, I'm going to be out making money and a better life for myself. What does it matter how this house has been built? I'll just be here to sleep. So what if it rains and drips a little on my head?*

But that doesn't work out very well for that pig, who becomes the wolf's dinner.

Pig #2 thinks, *Wow, is my brother dumb in using straw. Then again, he wasn't the sharpest tool in the shed at home. I know. I'll use sticks. They're tougher than straw, so they'll be harder for that wolf to tear apart. Besides, there are a lot of sticks around in the forest. I'll collect them and see what goes together. I'm sure I can come up with an arrangement that works.*

But that hit-or-miss method doesn't work out well for Pig #2. The Big Bad Wolf huffs and puffs and blows his house in. That pig becomes a tasty buffet for his enemy.

Then there's Pig #3. He sits awhile, thinking about the best approach for building the strongest of all foundations and houses. After gathering information from housing experts in the forest, like the beavers who are known for their craft, he evaluates the forest around him. What kinds of building tools and materials are readily available? What kinds of enemies might he face? What preparation does he need to do to protect himself and the future Ms. Piggy? And all those little piggies he'll have?

After careful consideration, he sketches up some drawings and decides on the best plan.

I need to use cement for a foundation and lace it with the strongest rebar. That way that nasty ol' wolf can't dig underneath and poke his head up into my living room. I'll make my own bricks for the walls with the toughest mortar I can find. And for the roof? I'll use a combination of dried-mud tiles and those tough vines that tenaciously grow everywhere and can't be killed.

That leaves only the chimney hole in the roof. As long as he keeps a fire going, no wolf will try to climb down his chimney to try to eat him or his family.

That very day Pig #3 toils sunrise to sundown until the center portion of his home is done and bricked in. When it starts to rain and a grumpy hedgehog outside is getting drenched, he invites Hedgy in to sleep by his fire. He is neighborly, after all.

The next day he checks the mortar to make sure it held up to the rainstorm and patches any damaged parts. He continues to work every day thereafter to keep his home solid and safe.

Meanwhile, the Big Bad Wolf is growing hungrier. His dinners of Pig #1 and Pig #2 have long worn off, and he's looking for Pig #3. But that stubborn pig won't let him in the door. He's not deceived by any disguises.

Finally, the Big Bad Wolf has had enough. He loses his patience. Stomach growling, he launches himself from a tree onto the roof and leaps down that chimney . . . right into the pig's pot of boiling stew.

The results for that wolf were too hot to handle.

Pig #3 was a master contractor who paid attention to his foundation. He got quality cement, the kind that won't crack easily in any kind of weather. He laced it with the strongest rebar to double that protection. His brick-and-mortar exterior was the best he could make, even though constructing it took time, unlike his two brothers' easier options. Without quality products, planning, and hard work, he knew that home, no matter how good it looked on the outside, wouldn't last or keep him and his family safe from predators.

What Pig #3 went through is a similar process parents go through in establishing a foundation when they wish to rear a child into a successful adult. In your home, you may have one or two master contractors, depending on whether you have a partner or are a single parent. You may also have some other home-builder helpers like Grandma, Grandpa, a sister or brother, or other extended family or friends who live with you or close by. Today's families come in all shapes and sizes.

What have you put into your foundation and your walls? Were those materials hastily cobbled together or carefully planned and constructed? Are they made of straw or sticks, easily destroyed? Or are they made of cement with rebar and the toughest bricks and mortar you can create?

The Three Cs

As you rear kids to become successful adults, you'll need what I call "the three Cs"—communication, compassion, and commitment.

Communication

Communication establishes the strongest possible foundation. If you and your partner don't decide together what qualities are the most important for your kids to have and stand united in pursuing them, look out. Those children of yours will find the cracks in your mortar and take advantage of that to unite against you.

If you hand down edicts to your kids—talking *at* them rather than *with* them—your foundation will be shaky indeed. It might work when they are younger and more easily controlled. But when they hit adolescence and mood swings and realize that their parents are far from perfect, look out.

Communication isn't one side talking and the other one listening. It's both sides talking, preferably one at a time, and both sides truly listening. Listening is an art form. You aren't really listening to the other person if you're spending the time she's talking figuring out what you're going to say next.

If you want to show your child you respect her, recognize her as an individual, value her opinions, and want to hear her perspective, you must be an attentive listener and an active participant in her life.

Rae, a mom who works full-time from home, is a good example. After her daughter Breana arrived, Rae took a pay cut to work from home. Breana grew up listening to her mother type as her lullaby, since she took her naps in her mom's home office, curled up in a cozy corner crafted especially for her.

When Breana woke up, the first person she'd see was her mother. Rae would stop working, pick up her daughter, and hug her. They'd talk eye to eye, even when Breana could only babble, and then do a fun project together.

Since Rae's family was on a limited budget, mom and daughter kept their projects and outings simple. They took walks together and kicked leaves. They learned about ladybugs and slugs at the public library and visited a free butterfly farm. They listened to music, made musical instruments out of wood, and danced in the kitchen. They colored eggs for fun when it wasn't Easter, had old-fashioned deviled eggs for lunch, and made mosaic pictures out of the eggshells.

> If you want to show your child you respect her, recognize her as an individual, value her opinions, and want to hear her perspective, you must be an attentive listener and an active participant in her life.

When Breana went to kindergarten, Rae set aside the hour her daughter got home from school as nonwork time. The two had tea, shared a snack, and talked about their days. Sometimes Breana had friends over to play. Rae would make creative snacks, like octopus hot dogs or tuna sailboats with toothpick flags. She didn't mind the splashes on the floor when her daughter and a friend decided to play "cat" and lick their milk out of bowls. Nor did she mind her lawn chairs disappearing under a mountain of leaves to become a "tunnel into another world" in the backyard.

Those mom-and-daughter chats lasted even through high school and morphed into FaceTime chats in college. Though Breana lives in another state now and is active in her new career, when she comes home, guess where she wants to take a nap? In her mom's office . . . because it's a reminder of warmth, home, and a mom who always took time for her.

Compassion

Compassion, an active consideration for the feelings and perspectives of others, is the mortar that holds together the bricks of your home. You and your child may go through the same event together but have varying responses. If Grandma dies, you feel sadness, regret, responsibility, or any other combination of emotions.

Your three-year-old twirly ballerina, though, doesn't yet understand death. Even if you tell her Grandma is dead and won't come over again, that won't compute. She'll only get upset because you're upset.

Remain calm and simply say, "Honey, I'm crying because I'm sad. When you're sad, sometimes you cry." You answer the questions that she asks—no more, no less. If she isn't satisfied, she'll ask for clarification. That's compassion: accepting her where she is in her understanding and not pushing for her to understand more unless she's ready.

Your pragmatic eight-year-old knows what death is. He already had a pet kitten die and knows that once something dies, it doesn't come back. He's accepted that inevitable fact and doesn't seem to get overly emotional. On the surface, his practical acceptance of death might make him look cold—like he doesn't care about his grandma. But nothing is further from the truth. Sometimes he crawls into his bedroom closet and cries.

Compassion is giving him a hug and saying, "Wow, I miss Grandma sometimes. And I especially miss her peanut butter cookies. I can still taste them." You smile. "But you know what? I have her recipe. Should we make some together?"

Then there's your 15-year-old caretaker. She's the one who had the most time with Grandma and took care of her when she needed help. She saw the decline in health as Grandma aged but didn't want to say anything, because she didn't want to worry you. She misses her grandma, but most of all she's worried about you. She's in overdrive mode trying to parent you. She takes care of the dishes and the laundry and skips her get-together with friends to come home and make dinner.

What does she need the most from you? To know that you'll be okay and she doesn't have to be your parent, watching out for you. And to know that it's okay for her to share her own sadness with you.

"I can't tell you how much I appreciate all you've done for me in the past few days," you say. "Grandma's death hit me hard. It must be difficult for you to see me cry. But you know what? Crying is okay when you're sad. It's like letting a bit of air out of a balloon so it doesn't pop. Each of us will be sad sometimes when we miss Grandma. That's normal. But you know what she always said: 'Tough times happen, but tough people still power on.' Well, I think of that and her every day. I'll be okay, honey, and so will you. All of us will. If you're ever sad, come find me. If I'm sad, I'll do the same with you. Is that a deal?"

You've opened the door to your daughter knowing it's okay and normal to grieve, and that you're willing to entertain her thoughts and emotions anytime.

Commitment

Commitment is what you do every day to make sure your foundation and walls stay secure. Then, no matter whether rain, sleet, snow, or sun hits your house, it remains strong and secure against enemies like the Big Bad Wolf.

How do kids spell commitment? It's simple: T-I-M-E. There's no such thing as quality time without quantity time. To build a strong foundation, you have to be involved in your kids' lives. Your actions must match what you say are your priorities.

How do kids spell commitment? It's simple: T-I-M-E.

Consistency in setting your children and partner as priorities over all else—a job promotion, a dinner with friends, or community events, to name a few—opens the doors to communication with your family members and liberally sprinkles those relationships with compassion. Your kids can't know how committed you are to them if you're not present with them.

Brad and Michelle had a three-year-old and a five-year-old. Both parents worked outside the home, while Michelle's sister, a stay-at-home mom with two kids of her own, watched the kids during the day.

Things changed when five-year-old Mikey said, "But, Daddy, how come *you* never play ball with me? Only Uncle Adam does."

That hit Brad hard. He realized that although he was in the midst of growing his career on the stock exchange, he was missing too much of his children's growing up. Michelle agreed.

Both parents decided to opt for flex time, where each of them worked from home one day a week. Tuesday became "Daddy day" to do special things with the kids, while Thursday became "Mommy day." Auntie had them the three other days, with Brad and Michelle switching off picking them up so that the other parent could work an extra hour at the office. The remaining hours of their 40- to 45-hour workweeks were done after the kids were in bed or were doing an activity with the other parent.

"I've never been busier," Brad told me, "but we're all happier. And I'm doing what matters most. I don't want to miss my time with the kids and regret it later."

The person your child needs most is you. Not the babysitter, the day-care worker, the after-school program director, the athletic director, or even Grandma or Auntie. Your arrangement won't look like Brad and Michelle's or anyone else's. All situations are unique, and you can get creative with mixing and matching. Just don't forget that your kids need to *see* your commitment to feel that they are a priority.

Without your presence, you can't catch teachable moments as they unfold.

Creating and Catching Teachable Moments

If you want to make sure your kids listen to what you say, don't lecture. Tell them stories. Use contemporary news to highlight qualities you want them to have. Your kids are constantly online anyway. You might as well put all that internet surfing to good use.

Teachable Moment Example #1

Is honesty important to you? Here's how Ed combined the day's news with a story from his growing-up years to make intriguing dinner conversation with his three kids.

"Did you see this morning's story about the high-school kids who cheated and got expelled?" Ed asked. "When I was in high school, I had a really hard physics teacher. Everybody hated him. Somebody circulated a test from his previous class to a bunch of my classmates. All you had to do was pay five bucks and you could get it too. But I didn't pay up because the whole thing seemed fishy to me. And my dad had told me that if something stinks like a fish, it probably is a fish you don't want to catch and eat.

"The kids who got the test got As. I got a D. It seemed so unfair. I was mad for a week. But a month later, one of them boasted about it, not knowing a teacher was in one of the bathroom stalls. All of those kids got caught and had detention for the last three months of school. The ringleader got expelled right before graduation. Boy, was I glad I didn't pay up and that I'd listened to that voice of my dad in my head."

You can lecture your child about being honest until the cows come home, but nothing carries that concept better than a real-life story, especially if it's about you. Tell them stories about the cool things you did, the risky things you did, and the stupid things you did. Believe me, they'll listen. You might even find them parroting what you said to their younger siblings.

Ed laughed when he told me he overheard his older son say to his younger son, "Are you really gonna fall for that one? You're smarter than that. You know, like Grandpa and Dad say, 'If it stinks like a fish, it probably is a fish you don't want to catch and eat.' Don't be an idiot."

> If you hear your own life stories emerging from your kids' mouths, you'll know you've done your job well.

Big brother took care of that life lesson swiftly before Papa had to offer any wisdom.

If you hear your own life stories emerging from your kids' mouths, you'll know you've done your job well.

Teachable Moment Example #2

While sitting at a restaurant, your family watches a waitress kindly handle a belligerent man. Finally he leaves, and the waitress approaches, asking for your family's order.

As she's apologizing for belatedly arriving, you smile broadly. "Not a problem. I'd say you had a lot on your hands a few minutes ago. I couldn't help but notice how pleasant you were to that man, who seemed quite angry. Your actions say a lot about the quality of person you are, and also about this restaurant for hiring you."

When you catch others being nice and give compliments where they're due, your children learn about professionalism, kindness, and seeing a situation from a holistic perspective . . . instead of only from the perspective of their growling tummies.

Even more, you've passed on a blessing. That waitress could have had a very bad day and gone home discouraged. Instead, she walked away smiling from your table.

Now that's good work all 'round.

Don't Forget the Basics

When you're prepping your kids for life, don't forget the basics. Courtesy never goes out of style. It amazes me how many people today were never taught to say these words and many others as they were growing up:

- "Please."
- "Thank you."
- "I appreciate that."
- "I'm sorry."
- "May I help you?"
- "Excuse me."
- "Would that be all right with you?"

In fact, business owners tell me they can't assume their new employees know the basic courtesies of how to treat their customers. They actually have to train them. Many of those employees also lack a hard-work ethic. They aren't equipped for the realities of everyday living, like understanding that you have to make more than you spend on rent, gas, and food, and that you need to leave a bit to pay Uncle Sam too.

When I founded the Leman Academy of Excellence, I wanted to make sure that kids were not only educated well in the traditional subjects of school but learned matters of the heart, like honesty, sharing, helpfulness, and kindness, as well as common courtesies. So, for example, we have an etiquette class where kids learn simple manners that can accompany them throughout life in any social situation.

When kids enter that class, I know what they're thinking:

- *This is dumb. Why do I have to know how to cook? I can just go out.*
- *Why do we have to learn which fork is used for what in a table setting? Who cares whether one is for dessert or salad or the main dish? Why can't we just use one fork or, even better, our hands?*
- *Seriously, I'm not two years old. Why do I have to learn to say please and thank you?*
- *This is embarrassing, role-playing what to do on a date.*
- *Do I really have to know what a corsage is?*

I can see the eye-rolls across the room.

But as class proceeds, they learn all sorts of fascinating things:

- Boys and girls are very different from each other. Girls have a wide range of emotions that can scare boys into becoming mutes or running for the hills. Boys tend to think, *Can I eat it, mate with it, or compete with it? Then I'm interested. Otherwise I'm good all by myself here.*
- Girls love to go potty in groups of 2, 4, 8, and 12—it's an event. Boys prefer to go it alone.
- Girls tend to be wordsmiths, comfortable with a flow of verbiage. Boys, who have a much lower word count by nature, sometimes barely get an "uh" out in response, especially if they really like the girl.
- Girls tend to mature faster than boys . . . in case you wondered why girls in your class often have their eyes on older boys.

Since boys are as dumb as mud when it comes to relationships (Seriously, aren't we? If you're a female reader, you're nodding), we role-play all kinds of scenarios in class, like these:

Scene 1: A boy really likes a certain girl. He asks a friend to go ask one of her friends if she might maybe like him, because he doesn't have the courage to do it for himself.

Girl's response: "If he wants to know if I like him, why doesn't he have the guts to ask me himself? Instead, he sends a posse. I'd never date anybody who's a chicken."

Scene 2: Three boys just discovered that girls are interesting aliens. Since they don't know how to approach those girls, they do what they'd do naturally to get other males' attention: punch each other and wrestle. They think they're being cool, impressing the socks off the girls.

The girls, viewing the spectacle, shake their heads and roll their eyes. *What idiots*, they think, walking away. *Who'd be interested in them?*

Scene 3: A boy wants to tell a girl he likes her. He walks right up to her, looks her in the eye, and says, "I like you. I think you're adorable."

Nope, that's not what he should do, or that girl will write him off as a nutcase.

Instead, he should talk with her, walk alongside her as she leaves class, and gently comment on something about her, such as, "Hey, you must like green. I've noticed that you wear it quite a bit. It looks good on you."

In a natural way, then, he could begin to form a friendship with her. During such a process he'll quickly discover if there's any interest on her part. That way he doesn't embarrass himself by plunging in with the "I like you" when there's no interest.

Scene 4: A girl is carrying a heavy bag.

A boy walks up alongside her. "Wow, that bag looks heavy. Could I help you with that? Or at least open the door for you?"

Such scenes are usually accompanied by nervous laughter in class and a few looks of *I can't believe we're doing this*. However, by the end of the class, those boys understand why what they learned is important. The "test" at the end is a dance. Those boys now actually know how to treat a young lady right and act like mature men you'd want your daughter to date.

Each boy graciously asks a girl to accompany him to a dress-up event, often with a handwritten invitation. He wears a suit, complete with a tie. He greets her parents when he picks her up, telling her mom and dad a little bit about his background and why he chose to "date" their daughter. He thanks them for the opportunity to accompany their daughter and says graciously, "I'll be sure to have her back by 11:00 p.m."

He pins a corsage on the girl without drawing blood or touching anywhere he shouldn't. Then he escorts his date out the door and slows his stride to match hers as they walk arm in arm to the car. Once at the car, he opens and shuts the door for her.

At the dance, he opens all doors for her, escorts her to their table, pulls out her chair, and seats her. When she and her friends get up to visit the ladies' room, all boys at the table stand, pull out their dates' chairs, and then seat their dates again upon their return.

He gently takes her hand to help her out of the car when they arrive at her home, walks her up the front steps, thanks her for accompanying him, and then bows to bid her adieu. He waits until she has entered her home before walking back to the car.

Now, don't you wish those Leman Academy of Excellence boys were the ones taking *your* teenage daughter out on a date?

If you want to rear a successful child, don't forget basic courtesies. Being able to carry those out in a very natural way will assist your child in every way down the line: in job interviews, college and career interactions, hiring a plumber, and even his gracious treatment of that person who might become your daughter-in-law someday.

When you teach your kids how to be kind, how to be respectful of others, and all the other virtues, you not only launch them toward life success, you do the world and their future families a great service.

Why not try some "practical living" training of your own? Toss out an idea for a situation during dinner. Ask, "Okay, if this situation happened, how would you handle it?"

Your kids will love to throw in their ideas, even if at first they're doing it only to one-up each other.

"Are you a doofus? You don't talk to a girl that way. There's a reason you're my *younger* brother."

"I'm a girl. Don't you think you should ask *me* how I'd want to be treated?"

And the banter will fly.

Soon your boring at-home meal will be filled with lively dinner conversation, and your kids will want more of it.

Trust me.

STRATEGY #6

STAY THE COURSE

Six "must" principles for sane parents to live by.

N othing good in life comes easy," my mom used to say. "You must stay the course."

When I was young, I rolled my eyes at those statements. All it meant was "Get to work, Cubby" (that was my nickname as a kid). It was a clever way to prompt me into doing something I didn't want to do, like my math homework, instead of going fishing at the local stream in upstate New York.

· But now that I'm older and much wiser, I understand that this statement applies to nearly everything in life. William Arthur Ward once wrote that the recipe for success is to "Study while others are sleeping; work while others are loafing; prepare while others are playing; and dream while others are wishing."[1] When your goal is to rear children into adults who will be healthy, balanced, hard-working, generous, and caring toward others and will contribute in a positive way to this world, it's a 24/7 job. That means you interact at the best of times and, frankly, at the worst of times.

Change of any kind requires staying the course when it's easy to do so and when it's hard to do so. When you provide foundational principles that are solid and unchanging in spite of the situation, your children have a safe base to operate from. As they grow older, they expand their area of experimentation, knowing that, succeed or fail, they return to a place where people love and support them. By allowing age-appropriate choices, you help them naturally curb their negative character traits and smooth off any rough relational edges, and you highlight and encourage positive qualities that pave their path to success.

As you raise your kids with that success in mind, remember the following six "must" principles to live by. They'll keep your perspective on the end goal and your sense of humor intact. Then you can skip expensive visits to a shrink or the spa to manage your stress.

Principle #1: Hold your child responsible and accountable for their choices.

We in America are into choices.

"McKenzie, it's 8:00. Have you chosen to go to bed yet? No? You want to stay up and watch TV? Well, Dad and I are going to bed. Just lock the front door and turn off the TV when you're done."

McKenzie, by the way, is only five years old. And yes, this did really happen. That girl, shorter than a yardstick, ran the show in her home. She had Mommy and Daddy wrapped around her pinkie in every way possible. She got away with it too. When she woke up cranky from lack of sleep, they bought her off with treats and then made excuses for her behavior in kindergarten.

Those parents needed an intervention, and fast. A few more years and that 38-pound princess would be a force to be reckoned with.

People sometimes think of order and discipline as restricting, negative words. However, they're both good when used in the proper context and with the right goals in mind.

163

If first graders are walking like ducklings in a row from the gym back to the classroom, with Mama Duck—aka the teacher—keeping them in line, then they're not shoving each other into lockers or giving each other swirlies in the drinking fountain. Most would consider that a plus.

There's a reason for order in families and for parents to act like parents and give children only choices that are appropriate. Children can't learn to become responsible without being given responsibility. And when they do make a choice, they need to be held accountable for it.

Let's say it's time for breakfast. You ask Buford, "Would you like Crispy Critters or Cheerios?"

Of course he says, "Crispy Critters," if for no other reason than the name sounds fun.

You pour the milk on those Crispy Critters in his bowl. But as soon as you do, what happens? He changes his mind. "I want Cheerios."

At that moment an authoritative parent does the smart thing. You allow that kid to live with the consequences of his choices. "You are more than welcome to choose Cheerios for breakfast tomorrow. But today you already made your choice. So Crispy Critters it is." Then you walk away and get busy doing something else.

Either the kid eats his choice of Crispy Critters or goes hungry for breakfast. Neither will kill him, and living with the consequences of a hasty choice is a good lesson.

If you can remember only one thing about this book, remember this: you can't recrisp a soggy critter. Once a choice is made, you can't undo it. You must live with the consequences.

You can't recrisp a soggy critter. You must live with the consequences.

The sooner your kids learn that, the better.

Consider this familiar scene. You're getting ready to drive your child to school in the ugliest four-door station wagon with black walls imaginable. I won't name the brand of the car, but you get the idea.

Your son gestures toward the car. "Really? Why couldn't we get a Camaro or a Mustang or something cool? I have to go to school in this?"

You shrug. "These wheels are a fact of life. But it's your choice to either get in or give those new athletic shoes of yours a three-mile workout."

He gets in. But a long distance away from school, he says, "Uh, you can drop me off here."

"We're still three-quarters of a mile away," you comment.

"I want to get out here," he insists.

You drop him off, knowing he's got a bigger hike than he thinks. Then again, it's his choice and he'll break in those new shoes quickly. If he's tired that evening from his extra exercise, so be it. Either he'll make a different decision the next morning, or he'll tone up any remaining baby fat and gain some muscle from his hikes.

Principle #2: Don't give away your authority cookie.

Parent, you were not put on this earth for your children to walk all over you.

Then again, neither were you put here to lord it over your kids like you're the king and they're the pawns on a chessboard.

If you take a look at the gimme generation, what are they saying by their behavior? "I'm in authority over you," not the other way around.

But let's be honest. Your kids wouldn't even have undies without you. They'd be going commando. And they certainly wouldn't have that cell phone or any of their other latest gadgets. So, who is fooling whom?

However, every time you allow a child to jerk your chain, you're allowing him to chip away at your authority. And if you have to

Dr. Leman's 10-Second Solutions

Q: My three-year-old never wants to eat anything at meals. If we put food on his high chair tray, he just stares at us as he pushes it off the edge. My carpet is a huge mess from the splatters. Finally, we give up and let him go play so we can at least eat in peace. How can we put a stop to such behavior?

A: First, invest in one of those thick plastic play mats or a painter's plastic sheet. You know, the easy-to-wipe-off variety. Make sure the whole area within slinging distance is covered, including the walls. That takes care of your carpet, unless it's already stained beyond repair, and any other objects in the vicinity. Now you can let the diminutive quarterback have free rein and practice his throwing skills. Just make sure you forewarn Grandma and Grandpa, who might be within range across the table.

Second, place the food on his tray as usual. If he pushes it off the tray or launches it, let it stay where it lands. But don't give him any more artillery to fire.

Third, don't react to his behavior at all. Don't say a thing. You clue in the rest of the family to ignore him completely, even if that is terribly difficult to do. He doesn't get out of that chair for any reason during dinner, no matter how much he vocalizes.

He's only behaving this way because it works. It gets your attention and makes him the center of that attention. If he has siblings, call it early sibling rivalry, if you wish. If that behavior no longer works to get him what he wants—whether it's to have a different kind of food, to get out of the hard high chair and onto your squishy, more comfortable lap, or to play with those toys he sees on the floor—he'll stop.

If this has been a pattern at meals, you need to stick with your plan to establish a new behavior. Eventually the natural consequence of hunger will win out when even the most determined slinger realizes, *Uh-oh. When I toss my food, it doesn't come back.*

Especially if his siblings are munching happily away at the other end of the table.

announce, "I'm in charge here. Do what I say," you're *not* the one in charge.

I want you to imagine that your parental authority is a cookie. Every time you react—take action without thinking—you are giving away a bit of that cookie. Every time you allow someone else to have authority over your child—whether a coach, teacher, summer camp worker, grandparent, or friend—you give away a bit of your authority cookie. You're letting others shape how your child develops.

> If you have to announce, "I'm in charge here. Do what I say," you're *not* the one in charge.

That's why you need to choose carefully who you're allowing to be around your child. Are those people role-modeling and teaching the qualities *you* want to teach them: the ones from your dream qualities list? Or are those people merely placeholders for the times you're not available, or perceived stepping-stones to the success you want your child to have?

Give too much of that parental cookie away and you end up with only cookie crumbles. And, as we all know, cookie crumbles don't have nearly as much of a draw as a whole cookie.

You should never allow your own reactions or others' authority over your child to chip away at your parental authority. Kids are smart enough to know who's in charge. So, who will it be: you or them?

Principle #3: Let reality discipline do the talking.

Directives like these from kids have incited revenge in parents for generations:

- "Back off."
- "Chill out."
- "You're in my space."
- "You're so stupid."
- "I hate you."
- "You don't have a clue."

And here's one of my favorites from my own growing-up years: "Don't have a cow, man."

I know it's hard when your adolescent's behavior screams, *Stay away from me. Get out of my life, out of my space. I need space.*

If you're the parent of a teenager, you've heard it all. What do you do when that barbed directive flies out of your kid's mouth? Do you get in that kid's face and say, "Do you know who you're talking to? I'm your *father [mother]*."

Well, you could, but you already know what happens when you do that. You escalate the situation for you and your child. Both of you end up angry, and you don't talk for days. The temperature in your home is either the Everglades in the middle of July or the Arctic in the middle of winter.

Do yourself a favor. Try something new. Don't react to those statements at all. Simply wait for a teachable moment.

Your teenage son walks up to you and says, "Uh, Dad, can I take the car? I'm meeting the guys."

You hear out his explanation. Then you shrug. "I'd like to help you, but right now I'm out of your life."

"What?" your son asks, confusion on his face.

"Well, this morning you said you were sick of me being in your life," you reply calmly. "I'm simply doing what you asked. I'm out of your life. And that includes the use of the car and anything else you need me to do for you."

That tactic will make any kid think twice before he opens his mouth and lets something rash fly out.

Reality discipline—letting the consequences do the talking for you, instead of you lecturing—works in every single one of these situations:

- Your son embarrasses you publicly with his vocal disrespect for you.
- Your daughter routinely lies. When you ask, "Who ate the last piece of cherry pie?" she says without thinking, "Not me"—even when she's holding a fork with the last bite of pie on it and there's a cherry stain on her lips.
- Your twins bite each other when they get angry.
- Your son says he was at his music lesson, but he wasn't.
- Your daughter has her hand out for money again. She already spent all her allowance for the week, and it's only Tuesday.
- Your son argues with you no matter what you say.
- Your daughter "forgets" to do her chores and goes to bed.
- Your son never admits to doing anything wrong. It's always his sister's fault.

Therefore, when those barbed directives fly out of your kids' mouths, do these two important things: close your mouth and remove yourself from the situation. If you can't remove yourself physically, remove yourself mentally. Think about your favorite

Dr. Leman's 10-Second Solutions

Q: My 11-year-old is so lazy. He never gets anything done, much less does anything on time. He's late to school half the time, and then he yells at me like it's my fault. How can I break that pattern?

A: Easy, and you can start as soon as the sun is up tomorrow. When he doesn't get up for school, don't be his alarm clock. Let him wake up on his own and do the mad scramble to get to school. Yes, you can drive him if you usually do or he missed the bus, but stay calm and don't engage in any of his fighting lingo or respond to his passing the buck of blame. Just call cheerily at the curbside, "Have a good day" and give a little wave, and then off you go into the wild blue yonder.

Don't write an excuse for him either. Getting chewed out by the office staff, teacher, and/or principal will be a memorable experience for that boy. Even better if you secretly prod that talk along with a call to the office: "I'm hoping you can help me with something. My son tends to be late to school, and I'm trying to curb that habit. If you could help me out by calling him in for a stern lecture, I'd greatly appreciate it." The folks in that office will think you're one smart cookie and be happy to oblige.

Your son may have a single bad day, but no doubt that boy will have learned something by the time he gets home, even if he's temporarily angry at you. After all, you're his pathway to food and everything he needs at this point in his life.

As for his other lazy activities, don't help him by doing things for him or reminding him. Let him take the fall for anything that isn't done. Natural consequences rule over parental tirades every time.

setting of blue skies, lapping waves on a beach, those fruity drinks with the little umbrellas . . .

Now don't you feel better?

I know that's simple advice, and it's much harder to do in the heat of the moment. But you need to be the adult in the situation, the one who hopefully has a broader perspective. If your child can't learn tolerance, patience, and how to express his frustration nicely from you, whom exactly will he learn it from?

Principle #4: Stick to your guns, but don't shoot yourself in the foot.

- "I told you not to do that. Over and over I told you. But you still do it. Are you stupid? Are you going to be stupid all your life?"
- "If you ever do that again, I'll ground you for a month."
- "I said no, and I mean no. Are you not listening to me? The next time you ask me something, I won't listen either."

We parents could get the Nobel Prize for issuing edicts we can't follow through on. When we do that without thinking, often we not only can't stick to our guns but also shoot ourselves in the foot.

When heated emotions engage, reactions cause us to make wild pronouncements or accusations that aren't true. We hurt feelings, overstate an issue, sidetrack the real issue, or throw out promises we can't or won't keep.

Just because a kid does the same thing over and over doesn't make him stupid . . . unless, of course, he's routinely getting zapped by sticking his finger in the electrical outlet.

All kids have selective hearing when it comes to their parents, probably because parents in general spew words too freely in their children's direction. Kids also have many plotlines going on in their heads when you tell them things. Do you hear everything your children tell you? Do you always remember everything everyone tells you? Neither do they.

Want your kids to listen to what you say? Try these tips.

Say things once. Then turn your back and walk away.

If you're not a continual font of verbiage, your kids are more likely to hear you. If you state your request once and don't follow it up with reminders, you're saying, "We respect each other, so we listen to each other. I only need to say it once, and I know you'll hear me."

If that child doesn't choose to hear you and hasn't finished her chores, she misses having ice cream with the family. If you told him you needed him to be in the car 15 minutes early and he didn't show, he doesn't make his soccer game.

Natural consequences will do the lecturing so you won't have to. You don't need to nag, raise your voice, or issue threats.

If your kids miss what you say this time, no doubt they'll listen more intently the next time you speak.

Make your "yes" yes and your "no" no.

There's nothing that makes a child more insecure than a waffling parent who says one thing and then changes his mind. If you say you'll be somewhere, be there. Don't let anything other than a tornado on your way home stop you. If you say you won't do something, then don't do it.

> Children thrive on routine and predictability, which create a zone of warmth and security in a topsy-turvy world.

Children thrive on routine and predictability, which create a zone of warmth and security in a topsy-turvy world.

Not everything in life is beneficial, nor is it healthy. If you draw clear guidelines and boundaries rather than spouting rules, it encourages your child to explore within a safety zone. When boundaries are set and a child knows what happens if she steps over those lines—natural consequences will follow and she won't be rescued—then the response is preset and always fits the situation.

It's never too much. It's never too little. As Goldilocks said in the classic children's tale, it's "just right."

Principle #5: Use this powerful two-letter word often: "NO."

I want you to try something. Go stand in front of a mirror. Practice this word: "No."

Say it again and again, until you can say it easily, with confidence. It's one of the most important words you'll ever say to your kids if you want them to be successful.

Some parents exhaust themselves trying to keep their hedonistic children happy. But what happens when that child you've done everything for gets out into the wider world? Others aren't going to run around like you do, trying to make your child's happiness their top priority.

"Yes" parents foster unhappy children who think the world owes them a favor. Unless you allow reality discipline to reign freely and stop rescuing your child from consequences, you'll create problems for your children that will crop up in their adult lives:

- They think they're never wrong. And when they're proved wrong, it's someone else's fault.
- They lie as a sheer matter of convenience.
- If they don't do a job well or finish it, they find an excuse.
- They argue for the sake of arguing and ruin relationships.

173

- They expect others to rescue them if they don't like doing a task.
- They're always the victim, never the perpetrator.
- They take from others but don't know the first thing about giving.
- Their drama-queen or king-of-the-hill behavior may initially draw a social network—for entertainment, if nothing else—but such drama will get old quickly if it involves their friends.

Painting life as a romp through the park is an illusion that won't hold up in the real world. That's why experiencing consequences now is the best thing that can ever happen to your child. It's not only okay if Muffy is unhappy, it's good. As I often say, "An unhappy child is a healthy child," because unhappiness prompts change.

Think about it this way. As an adult, you have the freedom to drive however you want and go wherever you want in your car. But if you drive southbound in a northbound lane, you're going to run into trouble and make yourself and others unhappy.

Your child, too, has freedom to do whatever he wants whenever he wants. However, when that behavior could harm himself or others or short-circuits developing traits he'll require for life success, he needs a driving lesson from you. Likely that lesson will make him unhappy.

- "No. You are not going to his house for an overnight. You have school tomorrow."
- "No. You didn't finish the work I asked you to do. You're not going anywhere until it's done."
- "No. You do not need a cookie. We're having dinner in half an hour."
- "No. I cannot buy you that. It's not within our budget."

Five Mantras Sane Parents Live By

1. Behavior is personal, but you don't have to take it personally.
2. Instead of reacting, just roll with it and let those chips fall where they may.
3. Don't act like you own your kids. They're only on lease to you for 18 years or so.
4. Thoughtlessly engage your mouth and your kids gain control.
5. Love unconditionally. Love always.

- "No. I can't help you with that right now. You have to wait because I'm helping your sister."
- "No. I can't read you a book right now. This is Mommy's quiet time and your quiet time."
- "No. I can't answer that question right now. I'm on the phone."
- "No. You can't drive the family car without us. You only have a learner's permit."

Say "No" when you need to. Say it calmly, with respect, and provide straightforward reasons, like the examples I gave above.

The sooner your child gets a taste of "No," the better. Remember, an unhappy child is a healthy child.

Principle #6: Be patient. All good things take time.

In the legendary movie *The Shawshank Redemption*, sentenced-to-life prisoner Andy Dufresne (played by Tim Robbins) spends 20 years using a small chisel to chip his way to freedom. To get to where he wanted to be—outside those walls that bound him—he needed to be persistent and faithful to his mission.

That's a good metaphor for parents too.

Some parents use sledgehammers to try to force their children to become successful in the way they think they should be. The process, for both them and their kids, is like trying to force a

How My Life Changed: Aidan's Story

As a dad of two teenagers, I used to easily blow up when they threw disrespectful comments my way, and I'd give 'em right back. Needless to say, we didn't get along.

But I've been doing things differently for the past month, just like you suggested. Last week my 14-year-old got mad at me for not giving her $20 and yelled, "You're so dumb. You'll never understand."

Instead of giving her the usual what-for, I said, "Yup, you're right. Sometimes I am dumb. But you can always try me with any explanation. Find me when you want to talk. I'll be ready to listen."

Then I left the room. When the kitchen got quiet, though, I couldn't help myself. I peered around the corner.

My daughter looked confused. When her brother entered the kitchen, she said, "Uh, I think there's something really wrong with Dad. Does he seem different to you? I mean, the whole last month he's been acting kind of crazy."

That revelation was the start of the transformation in our house. It took three weeks of me being consistent for the idea of change to kick in. But after that, my kids and I started having decent conversations.

You were right. The change had to start with me.

square peg into a round hole. It doesn't fit comfortably because that technique doesn't work and the hole is the wrong shape of success for the child.

Other parents use Q-tips to brush the dust off their kids and try to smooth their rough edges, when sometimes good ol' sandpaper is needed.

But smart, entrenched-for-the-long-haul parents realize that everything good takes time. Rearing a successful child in a "whatever" generation will take a lot of persistence and faithfulness. You won't always like your child, and she won't always like you. But staying in control of your emotions and being consistent in your parenting style, while allowing age-appropriate choices and letting natural consequences fall where they may, allow you to ride out the ups and downs of the journey like a seasoned pro.

All of us are creatures of habit. It takes a while to carve a new path, especially if it's different from any path you've taken. That's especially true if you've had the wrong tools in your hands for a while. Maybe you've been using the same techniques your parents used with you. Those things you claimed you'd never say or do, you're saying and doing. Or because of your own rough upbringing, you've tried too hard to befriend your kids instead of being their parent.

As much as you'd wish otherwise, some kids will go their own way for a while. But if you practice authoritative parenting and use reality discipline, your children will develop responsibility and accountability. Consequences are natural teachers. Whether your kids learn the easy way or the hard way is up to them.

Do you hold your child responsible for her actions? Is she accountable to manage specific tasks and adhere to a timetable for doing them? The best way to open the door to changes in attitude, behavior, and character is to start with an open, honest, even-keeled conversation.

Life isn't a fairy tale with a wrapped-up ending, as much as we'd like it to be sometimes. It's real, with a lot of messy episodes interspersed. But you can start from where you are right now with these three simple ideas:

1. Give age-appropriate responsibility.
2. Allow the child to make his or her own choice.
3. Hold the child accountable for that choice, including any consequences.

Parenting a successful child isn't easy, but it is simple. Change yourself, change your child.

That is an iron-clad promise.

STRATEGY #7

MINIMIZE FRICTION, OPTIMIZE SOLUTIONS

How you can get your kids to listen every time.

"No matter what I say, he has to argue."

"She's so spacey. She would forget her own head if it wasn't attached to her body."

"I didn't realize until now how spoiled my kid is. My mom warned me I was spoiling him, but did I listen? No, and now I'm paying for it."

"My kids fight and fight and fight. It's a daily routine that's really getting on my nerves. No matter what I say or do, they still fight."

"The one thing she's good at is making trouble. She doesn't always mean to—at least I don't think she does—but she makes lots of messes I have to clean up."

"He does listen to what I say. But he does the opposite to spite me."

"If that kid tells me no in that tone one more time, I'm gonna blow and do something I'll regret."

"I worry about her because she can't take life seriously, ever."

"He's kinda aimless. Like a car that wanders all over the road instead of driving in one lane. The rest of the family? We're in the fast lane."

"Since she turned 13, we haven't had a single conversation that didn't end in yelling or an icy standoff. What gives?"

"He's so into his friends, he's forgotten his family exists."

These are only a few of the myriad comments I've heard from parents who want real solutions to the friction they're feeling between themselves and their kids.

We all love our kids, but let's be honest. Sometimes our sheep are hard to like, aren't they? They're inconvenient and messy, and they sometimes venture off the path of our leadership and get themselves stuck in thorny bushes. We then have the painful and annoying job of extracting them.

On top of that, there's always one lamb who's a troublemaker, that child who gets on your nerves. Sometimes you have to temporarily cull him from the herd in a time-out to bring him back into line since he causes problems for the flock in general. At your worst moments, you're tempted to make lamb chops out of him.

You know what I'm talking about. As soon as you hear that kid's footsteps down the hallway, you know another head-to-head is likely.

What Most Parents Do

When there's a clash between parent and child, most parents choose one of two actions.

Choice #1: You pacify your kid with words, action, or stuff and give in to those unruly demands. Your motto? Peace at any price. In short, you buy that kid off.

Problem is, that peace is short-lived until the next escapade. Is that really what you want? Or do you want to end that clash right now? If so, you have the power to end it. I'll show you how in this chapter.

Choice #2: You take him on head-to-head, determined to win. You dig in on your position and tell yourself, *This kid is not going to get away with what he's doing. Doesn't he realize who I am? I'm his* mother. *I pushed for nine hours to give that kid life. There's no way I'm gonna be treated this way.* Therefore, you give him what he wants. You engage in battle.

But if you engage in battle or in playing a game with a headstrong child, you will lose. You have much more to lose than he does, because that kid has an uncanny ability to know when he has you stretched over the proverbial barrel.

> If you engage in battle or in playing a game with a headstrong child, you will lose.

You have a reputation to protect in public. You don't want to be embarrassed in front of your friends, colleagues, or relatives. But you're also in the parental role, and you don't want to embarrass him in front of his friends or anyone else since that could "permanently damage his psyche." You're not entirely sure what a psyche is, but you've read about it in a bunch of parenting blogs.

Consider this conversation I had with Jolene, a mom of three children. Nine-year-old Melody, her oldest, was running her around the block emotionally.

"She was always a fussy baby, crying a lot and getting frustrated easily," Jolene told me. "As she grows up, those tendencies are getting even stronger. She's only nine, but she says things like, 'I wish I could go live with another family. I'm ugly. I hate myself.' I try to tell her those things aren't true and reinforce the good things. But nothing seems to sink in or work."

"Why do you think she says things like that?" I asked. "Any idea?"

"Well, I definitely react when she says them. I grew up in a household that was pretty rough, and I often wanted to leave home. But I never said that. I didn't dare. I feel bad when my daughter says it."

"Another question for you, then. How has life been unfair to her?" I asked.

Jolene frowned thoughtfully. "It hasn't. She's had a very good life. She has us and lots of things, and she's not ugly. I don't know where she gets all these ideas from."

I smiled. "I do. You have a power-driven child who has discovered the best way for you to pay attention to her. She knows your buttons to push, and she's an expert at pushing them. You're overidentifying with her. Since you had a rough childhood, you want to smooth her pathway so she doesn't experience the same things. But she's not in the same setting. She has a good home.

"To get and keep your attention, which is now divided between her and your two younger children, she's figured out the road map. *All I need to do is tell Mom, 'I'm no good. I'm ugly. I'm this. I'm that,' and I can get her to pay attention to me and give me anything I want.* That's a setup for you to say, 'Now, Melody, why do you say that? You're such a beautiful girl. You're good at . . . ,' and you go on to lather on praise, even some that isn't deserved, in an attempt to make her feel better about herself.

"That girl is playing you, and you're falling for it. Even more, you're the only one who feels bad about it. Melody will continue doing that until her behavior no longer works. Instead, try this: the next time she launches into her woe-is-me tirade, say, 'Melody, I'm sorry you see yourself that way. I'll tell you the truth: I don't see you that way. But what you think and feel is up to you. I can't change that.' Then you turn your back, walk away, and get busy doing something else."

182

Dr. Leman's 10-Second Solutions

Q: I'm tired of the door slamming in our house. Sometimes it's intentional, when my kids are mad about something. Other times it's just carelessness as they enter or leave our home. Still, the banging sound is the same. How can I put a halt to that headache-inducing activity? It's driving me nuts.

A: That's nothing a screwdriver couldn't fix, even if you have to borrow one from a neighbor. If it's your kid's bedroom door and he likes to slam it for effect, take that puppy right off its hinges and let the free-flowing breeze begin. Kids love their privacy. When it comes to shutting their door more quietly and having some privacy, or having no privacy at all, 9.9 out of 10 kids will take the first option.

Then again, if it's your door to the outside, removing it is probably not an option.

You could try a sense of humor: "Oh, I missed it. Try slamming the door again, but harder this time. I bet the whole neighborhood would enjoy it." That's better than barking, "Do you think we live in a barn? Close that door like you live in a house."

Or you could quietly pull aside that child who is slamming the door unintentionally and say, "I'm wondering if you could do something for me. I need your help." You wait until the child's eyes meet yours. "The sound of a door slamming really bothers me. It interrupts my work, makes me jumpy, and gives me a headache. I'd really appreciate it if you could take a second to hold the door so it shuts more quietly whenever you go in or out. I'm asking everyone in the family to help out."

If you have multiple door slammers in the family and want to add some zest to the problem solving, have a Door Slam Jar. Every time one of you catches someone else slamming the door, the offending party has to put a quarter or a buck in the jar. At the end of the month, the kid who has been caught slamming the door the least gets the booty in that jar to spend on whatever he wants.

Let the *good* sibling rivalry begin.

"Do you really think that will work, Doc?" Jolene asked.

I grinned. "I *know* it'll work. It has for hundreds of thousands of parents who've faced the same issue. Try it for yourself and see."

Three weeks later, an ecstatic Jolene wrote, "Wow, it really worked. Our entire family is happier since we no longer have a constant rain cloud in our home."

If your child is pulling your chain, it's time to disconnect the chain. But you have to be consistent. Say something once, and then don't reengage in the game. Walk away. When no one is playing on the other side, games get old and boring fast.

Why You and That One Particular Child Clash

There's something else I want to point out about Jolene and Melody. The reason Jolene had trouble disengaging from her daughter's emotions is because she had grown up feeling ugly, hating her surroundings, and wishing she could live somewhere else. Jolene couldn't stand the idea that her daughter could grow up just like she did as a firstborn, thinking and feeling the same things.

Her own emotions hampered her from realizing that her daughter's setting was far different from the one Jolene grew up in. On top of that, Melody didn't really feel ugly. She was merely using the words she knew would trigger her mother's attention and empathy. The trap was effective until Jolene decided to disengage.

Think for a second about the kid you clash with most. It'll take only a second, because she's easy to pick out. She's the one who raises your blood pressure with her words and antics.

But who is that kid really? She is the one *most like you*. That's why the two of you are like rams butting horns over territory. Both of you are entrenched in your positions, and neither of you wants to move. She can easily push your buttons, even ones you didn't know you had. However, when you understand who she is, who you are, and why the two of you react to each other the way you do, you can then respond in a positive way to that child and life's surprises.

Why Your Bear Cubs Are Different

Amazing how your cubs can come out of the same den—your home—and be so different, isn't it? Though each of us has our own set of fingerprints, I've learned through years of studying birth order that we can get some clues about how firstborns and only children, middleborn children, and babies of the family will respond to life and each other.

I'll use the Leman family I grew up in as an example. May and John Leman had three cubs: Sally, Jack, and Kevin.

My sister, Sally, is eight years older than me. She's a class act—the kind of person who even ties bows on garbage bags before she takes out the trash. When you arrive at her home, the first thing that greets you at the door is a clear vinyl runner, from which you can choose the path to any room. You go in, hang a left, and enter the living room, and then you see the sheets over the furniture

185

that isn't being used so it doesn't get dusty. She alphabetizes her spice rack and irons the doilies on the davenport for pleasure. Her children were color-coordinated from the day they emerged from the womb. She would even put newspaper under her cuckoo clock if she had the opportunity.

But that's my firstborn sister: a student, achiever, and perfectionist who has everything under control. The one who married a firstborn dentist whose motto is, "Find the hole, drill the hole, fill the hole." Oh, and then, "Bill the hole."

Next is my brother. He was a typical rough-and-tumble middle child, yet also the firstborn boy who got my father's name. John Jr. was called "Jack," though, so my mom wouldn't mix up the two names when she was calling them for dinner. He was my big brother, and I worshiped him. A star quarterback of his high-school football team, he was also voted best looking at the senior prom and had a host of other accolades. I still remember wearing his number 12 jersey at school when he was a senior and I was in eighth grade. I felt like Hercules, standing on top of the world in Jack's shirt.

Then along came little Kevin, aka "Cubby." I'm the one who applied to 140 colleges and universities and couldn't get into any of them. Not a one. I even applied to my church denomination's school and they turned me down. Even though I sent them a Scripture about forgiveness, they were unimpressed. To this day, decades later, I remember their response:

> Most regrettably, Kevin's record does not support admissions. Rather, therefore, than grant him probationary admission which our studies show would lead to his failure, we must decline his application.

When I got the letter, I called my brother excitedly. "Jack, I got into college. I got the letter right here."

"That's wonderful," he said. "Where? Let me hear the letter."

I read it to him.

He laughed. "You didn't get in, stupid. They turned you down."

That's how out of it I was as a 17-year-old. I was taking consumer mathematics at the time, trying to figure out how many apples I'd have if I started with three and someone ate two of them.

I look back at my lack of drive then and shake my head. I had no idea what I was doing, much less where I was heading. No wonder I used to drive my teachers and parents up the wall.

With that as a background, do you see why I believe that *every child* can succeed in life? You, parent, just have to help them find the right formula.

Who Your Child Really Is

You might think each of your children came out of the same den, but they actually didn't. That's because with the addition of each child to your household, the makeup of that den changes.

Here's what it's like for each of your kids as they enter your family. To highlight the differences, we're going to put each of your kids in the same setting. Imagine you're on a family vacation by the ocean. Listen to the waves. Breathe in that salty air. . . .

Your Firstborn

This kid stands on the beach and surveys his surroundings. He's searched the internet for the temperature, the wind velocity, the potential for rain for the day, and when the tides come in and out in that area. He puts down his beach mat in a strategic position. His towel, sunglasses, and suntan lotion are all carefully organized on one side of the mat, with his sandals holding down the other side.

When he finally gets to the water, he shakes his head at his younger siblings, who are already cavorting in the ocean. With an eagle eye toward his possessions back on the beach, he does a shimmy step into the water, trying to figure out where the drop-off is.

Firstborns are organizers, list makers, and planners. They have to have lists to find their lists. They know exactly how things ought to be done and believe there's a right way and a wrong way to do things, with no in between. Thus, others can see them as bossy. But it's all because they fear errors and hate surprises.

Firstborns are groomed from babyhood onward for success. They are the benchmark of the family and the responsible ones you can count on. That's why they get the most frequent parental lectures:

- "What was that? How could you treat your *little* brother like that?"
- "I don't care what she did. You're the oldest. I expect more from you."
- "You don't want to take your brother with you? Fine. You can stay home."

Firstborns get assigned the most chores too, since they're the ones who will always get them done. It's no wonder they become achievement oriented and are cautious about new experiences, like jumping into water without knowing the depth of it. They see themselves as counting in life only when they win, compete, and dominate.

Firstborns are groomed from babyhood onward for success.

Of the first 23 astronauts in space, 21 were firstborns and 2 were onlyborns. Note there wasn't a single middleborn or baby in the bunch. Firstborns become librarians who shush you, architects who draw up houses that will stand up against any storm, accountants who will find the one flaw in your taxes, engineers who build lasting roads, and airline pilots you trust to get you up into the air and down in one piece.

Your Onlyborn

This child acts like a firstborn but is even more careful and perfectionistic. It takes him twice as long to calculate everything the firstborn would and to wade cautiously into that water. Depending on his age, he might ask you to go with him, even if there are lots of kids his age on the beach. After all, he's more comfortable interacting with adults because he's used to being with only his parents.

Only children are in a class all by themselves. They often get a bad rap as being spoiled, but let me assure you most of what they're accused of isn't true. Actually, onlyborns have all the traits of firstborns, but in triplicate. While firstborns are conscientious and reliable, only children are super-conscientious and super-reliable. Want a job done? Hire an only child. They're worth their weight in gold. They'll stay up all night to get it done.

Onlies feel even more parental pressure because not only are they the benchmark for their families, they're the *only* mark. Therefore, if they mess up, the whole family reputation is toast. That makes onlyborns additionally cautious, competitive, and highly allergic to mistakes.

They also can be extremely fearful. Because there's only one of them, they wonder, *What if Mom or Dad dies? What if I'm the only one left?* This is even more true if they were adopted and have experienced abandonment already, or if they're a stepchild who experienced the betrayal or death of a parent.

> Only kids often get a bad rap as being spoiled, but let me assure you most of what they're accused of isn't true.

Only children have a particularly quirky trait: they can't understand why siblings fight. Just ask Maria, an onlyborn who married into an Italian family of four brothers.

189

Your Middleborn

From the instant this child hit the beach, she's scoping for other kids her age to hang out with. She has no problem searching them out and leaving that bossy older brother or younger scalawag brother behind. Within five minutes, she's found a new group to hang out with and is soon tossing a Frisbee with them. You barely see her the rest of the day except for when she runs back to scoop up some of your snacks.

If there's one Midas guarantee of birth order, it's that the first two children in any family will be day-and-night different. The secondborn watches the way the firstborn has gone and says, "No way can I compete with that, so I'm gonna do the opposite."

Say to any middle child the words "family photo album," and you're going to get an eye-roll. That's because most families have thousands of pictures of the firstborn in gold-leaf albums. The middle child? She might have four pictures of just her. Likely her first picture in life is with her brother or sister's arm over her head. She doesn't have many without her siblings intruding on her thunder.

> If there's one Midas guarantee of birth order, it's that the first two children in any family will be day-and-night different.

That's why middleborns are used to fending for themselves and creating social networks outside of your home. You might not notice they're missing from home for a while since they're not in your eagle-eye view, like your firstborn, or demanding your attention, like your baby. However, they reign as king or queen in their social circles because they're loyal friends whom others can count on. Secretive themselves, they carefully guard others' secrets.

Middle kids are used to wearing hand-me-downs, especially if their older sibling is the same sex. They're masterful negotiators between their warring siblings, if for no other reason than to create some peace for themselves. Because they hate confrontation and being squeezed between their siblings, they tend to compromise.

One of the US presidents known for his diplomacy in negotiating foreign affairs was Richard Nixon, a middle child. Abraham Lincoln and John F. Kennedy were also middleborns. Contrast that with the fact that most of our presidents have been firstborns. Only a few babies of the family have made it to the White House, since the majority are obviously like me: they'd get lost on their way *to* the White House. There was William Henry Harrison, who lasted one month in office,[1] and Andrew Johnson. Neither were the most prestigious presidents we've had. The most famous baby of all was Ronald Reagan. His wife Nancy, an only child, called him "Ronnie." (For the record, firstborns and babies make great marriage matches. For more on this and other marriage matches, see *The Birth Order Book: Why You Are the Way You Are.*[2])

Your Baby of the Family

As soon as this kid sees the sparkling water, he drops his beach towel and flip-flops in a heap—never mind where they land. Yelling, "Shazam!" with arms flailing wildly, he charges at the water and jumps right in. It doesn't matter that a big whitecap is heading directly toward him. He lets it engulf him, then spurts up out of the water like a dolphin, grinning widely.

Once he charges out of the water, he sees kids his age building a sandcastle and easily inserts himself into the group with his charming ways. Ten minutes later he brings the whole group back to your picnic feast to help themselves and sits in the middle of the action, loving every minute of it. Excitement and adventure are your baby-of-the-family's middle names.

Babies use cuteness to get away with murder. A baby's favorite game is getting an older sibling in trouble by taunting him. Since big brother isn't going to take that from a pipsqueak sibling, he will pound on him. What happens next? Baby kicks up a big fuss.

Mama or Papa Bear rips that door open. "All right, what's going on in there?" They eye the older sibling. "How many times have I told you to leave your little brother alone?"

A baby's favorite game is getting an older sibling in trouble.

Meanwhile, Schnooky is crying because big brother Moose hit him. But inside, what is that baby saying? *Ha, you poor sucker. I gotcha.*

Babies are social and charming. But they're also manipulative. They could sell rats for a living if they had to, or get their siblings to do their chores anytime they wish if they play their cards right. I ought to know. I'm a baby of the family, and I knew how to work it so my sister, Sally, or brother, Jack, did what I should have done.

What Your Kids Need Most from You

Because your kids are different, what they each need from you to feel special isn't the same. Birth order rules in your home, whether you've recognized it or not up until now. Firstborns tend to have the most responsibility, while babies go scot-free. Middleborns get hammered or ignored from both sides.

As I said earlier, for kids to become responsible, they have to be given responsibility. That means *all* your kids should have jobs and be accountable for doing them. As the firstborn gets busier with school and other activities, his responsibilities at home should lessen instead of increase. Some of his jobs should get passed down to the younger kids, who then need to step up to the plate.

Above all, do *not* have your kids work in the same area of the house or yard. Otherwise what happens will be predictable. The firstborn will get frustrated with the lackadaisical baby's organization and take over her work. The middleborn will slip out of the yard and into the neighbors' yard, where his friends are already gathered. And the baby will be . . . well, somewhere else that is definitely not the work zone you requested.

Your Firstborn or Onlyborn

Here are the top three things your firstborn or onlyborn needs from you:

1. *Reasonable expectations.*

   Don't hold a carrot out so far that your child can't reach it. If she does reach it, don't move it out farther. She already expects a lot of herself. Don't add to her burden. It's one thing to expect excellence from your kids; it's another to expect perfection.

   If standards are out of reach, your child will never think she's good enough for you. That is not a recipe for long-term success if you push her to go to Harvard and she manages to make it in, but then she is confronted with a bunch of other high-achieving young people just like herself whom she has to compete with.

2. *Job relief and perks related to their position.*

   Don't always call on your firstborn to do jobs that you want done and done right. Your other kids have legs and arms too. Your middleborn and baby need to learn how to take responsibility and be accountable for assignments they don't complete. Your firstborn shouldn't be the expected last-minute family babysitter when yours falls through. That is, unless she doesn't have other plans and agrees to it. If so, she should receive compensation, such as the money you'd set aside for that babysitter, or a trade, like getting to have her friends over the next weekend for a movie night.

   The firstborn who puts up with younger siblings trashing his bedroom and embarrassing him in front of friends deserves a few perks, like a slightly later bedtime or a corner of the basement where siblings aren't allowed to intrude. That says to him, "Listen, I know your brother and sister can be pesky sometimes. Because you put up with a lot, including times I give you too much to do, I want you to have some time when your siblings aren't allowed in your space." A bedtime half an hour or an hour later will work wonders on how your firstborn feels about his siblings.

3. *Grace.*

If you have a firstborn or only child who starts projects but doesn't finish them, rips up pictures he's drawn, or does homework but doesn't turn it in, that's a sign of discouragement. However, it's also a sign of something else: that there's at least one critical-eyed parent in the house.

A critical-eyed parent, the kind who can spot a flaw at 200 paces, is a firstborn's and only child's worst nightmare. Perfectionism is slow suicide. Your child *will* fail, just as you fail, because he is a human being. He needs the same grace that you'd want extended to yourself. He also needs to know, "It's okay not to be perfect. You don't have to get all As or secure the lead in the class play or get a spot on the basketball team. I love you just the same."

Your Middleborn

Here are the top three things your middleborn needs from you:

1. *To be noticed.*

Think for a minute. Who is the kid with the worst position in the family? It's your middle child. You have the firstborn achiever and the apple-of-his-parents'-eye baby (whether you want to admit it or not). Then there's your middle daughter, who has a tough act to follow on both ends. She'll never ask for attention, but she needs it as much as the others.

Go out of your way to catch her doing good things, and compliment her on them. "You are amazing. I appreciate the way you stay calm under crisis, even when your brothers are firing missiles at each other. You always seem to find a way to get them to see reason. Nobody else in our family is as good at that as you."

2. *To be asked for their opinion or advice.*

Middleborns are used to playing mediator and compromiser between sparring siblings. But they're not used to being asked for advice. In fact, they're the least likely to be asked their opinion, at least at home. So why not solicit your middleborn's opinion on something he's good at?

If your 11-year-old son is an internet whiz, say, "Hey, I'm really struggling with some internet research. You're good at it. Would you be willing to take a few minutes to help me?"

Asking your child for help is saying, "I acknowledge that you're good at this. I'm paying attention to what you're good at. And I think you make a unique, valuable contribution to this family." Such affirmation tells a middleborn that he's important and spurs him on to suggest other areas he could help you with, growing his own skills.

So, ask for his opinion on family events, since he's the least likely to speak up about where to go for dinner, have a picnic, or go on vacation. If he's good at math, let him help out on family finances.

3. *To have time alone with you, without their siblings.*

Middle children need special attention so they don't slip through the cracks.

What does your middle child like to do? If your 15-year-old likes to ski, take her by herself for a fun weekend.

Leave the other two kids at home, as much as they yell, "That's not fair. You're taking *her*? Why can't we go?"

Do her another favor. Take pictures of just her on that wonderful outing, and other times too. Save yourself some embarrassment. That way, down the road you don't have to say to her potential partner, "Uh, a picture of just her? Well, we have some family pictures, if you'd like to see those."

Your Baby of the Family

Here are the top three things your baby of the family needs from you:

1. *To be noticed and appreciated.*

    Babies live for their time in the limelight. They're the entertainers who make you laugh and take the edge off tense situations by their presence. However, if they're ignored or not appreciated for their skills, they can quickly become discouraged and resentful. A discouraged baby won't have any motivation. A resentful baby can cause you a heap of trouble.

    Try this: pretend like your baby of the family is a seal performing in a show at a zoo. All he needs to perform his best is an audience and a fish or two of appreciation once in a while. Then you'll be stunned at what that baby can do.

2. *To be held responsible and accountable.*

    Because babies are charming and can be manipulative, they're very good at wiggling their way out of work by talking siblings into doing it. Or they drop the ball, knowing someone else in the family will sigh and say, "Oh, brother, that's Suzy," and do it themselves instead of tracking the pixie down.

Babies of the family need responsibility in order to learn responsibility. They need to be accountable for when they drop that ball or don't see a task through to the end. The worst thing you can do for babies is rescue them.

You should never do anything for your kids that they should do for themselves.

> **You should never do anything for your kids that they should do for themselves.**

3. *To realize that others matter.*

Because babies love the spotlight, they sometimes forget that they can't always be the one in it. Your other kids deserve time there too. Many babies are raised to think they're the sun every other planet revolves around. It's not so, and the sooner they learn that, the better for their success in life and for everyone around them.

But here's some wonderful news. Babies are loving, affectionate, generous people who make friends quickly. When they realize that others matter, they can be a networking dream for companies who know how to handle and motivate them.

When you understand who your kids are and what they need most from you, you can avoid those clashes that turn your home into a war zone. Minimizing friction and optimizing solutions help focus your energy where it counts: motivating your kids toward success in the ways that match their worldview and gifts.

For more intriguing information on birth order and the variables that affect the family constellation, such as gender, age spread, and role reversals, check out *The Birth Order Book*.[3] What you learn will change your family life in ways you can't imagine.

Dr. Leman's 10-Second Solutions

Q: My third son backs off every time anyone challenges him on even the smallest thing. How can I teach him to stand up for himself? He's going to need that to survive among his pack of three brothers, much less in this dog-eat-dog world.

A: If that quieter, gentler boy is growing up with three brothers, it's honestly a miracle he's lived this long. A passel of boys can be a tough crowd. That's an awful lot of competition and arm wrestling to live up to.

Your third son is likely squashed between two older brothers who are stars in their own right and a younger, entertainer-type sibling. If one of his older brothers is the academic star, the other is probably an athletic or music star. That leaves son #3 in a murky no-man's-land, not sure who exactly he's supposed to be. He certainly can't and doesn't want to compete with his older brothers or that baby of the family, who has loud and annoying down pat.

Son #3 is likely the one who will go missing from the dinner table and not be noticed. Yet, ironically, he's the one all the brothers run to when they have a fight. That's because your "back-off" boy has a natural gift for mediation, and he's developed it into a fine art with his brothers. Outside your family, that gift has helped him form a loyal pack of friends who will stick together and protect each other.

Not every kid has to be a fighter like your other boys to survive in this world. We need mediators and entertainers too.

Here's what your boy needs:

- to know that his opinions, thoughts, and feelings matter.
- to have one-on-one time with you, without his brothers.
- to see your specific interest in him and his activities.
- to hear often what you appreciate about him.
- to know his particular gifts are not only needed but wanted in your family. No one can take his place.

Do those things, and son #3 will hold his head up high and stand up for himself, even among that overwhelming mass of testosterone in your home.

Blessings upon you all.

Six Practical Solutions to Minimize Friction

Whenever two or more humans share the same space for long periods of time, there's bound to be some friction. Learning how to minimize that irritating friction is critical to your goal of raising a successful child. When you respond calmly to behaviors that normally would turn your words into ballistic missiles, that transformation will prompt your kids to scratch their heads, wondering what's happened to good ol' Mom or Dad.

Kicking off any transformation starts with you. When your kids see that you are consistently doing things differently, they'll be drawn like cats to catnip and will want to know why.

Following are six practical solutions to minimize irritating friction.

#1: Ask yourself, "What will I do differently this time?"

Do a bit of self-evaluation. When a particular situation happened before, what did you do?

Did that work?

Likely not, or that situation wouldn't occur again.

Since that method didn't work, ask yourself, "What will I do differently this time for a different outcome?"

However, such questions don't work unless you have your road map in mind. That's why the first thing I had you do in this book was decide on the character traits you feel are important for your child to develop in order to become a successful adult.

For example, if honesty is a critical trait to you, and your eight-year-old steals a candy bar from a convenience store, you'll want to nip that in the bud fast. You won't hammer the kid for his action, but you'll make your feelings clear: "We're Smiths. And Smiths do not steal. It's wrong to take something that belongs to someone else and that you didn't pay for."

You won't let the kid off the hook by saying, "I'm sure he didn't mean it. He's only eight. He probably didn't know it was wrong." Even an eight-year-old knows the clear difference between right and wrong. If he didn't, why did he eat that candy bar in secret and try to stash the wrapper where you wouldn't see it?

That kid isn't as dumb or innocent as you think.

So do the right thing. March that kid back to the convenience store, even if it causes you temporary embarrassment as a parent. You don't rescue him. You stand behind him, but *he* does the talking to the manager. It is *his* piggy bank that takes the hit to pay for that candy bar. And if the manager decides he owes double or needs to do some work to pay for his crime of stealing, then so be it. Wouldn't you rather your eight-year-old learn about honesty now, before he decides to "borrow" a clothing item when he's 13 or a car when he's 16?

Don't be afraid to suffer a bit of embarrassment now for your child's long-term good. When you do things differently, your child will know you mean business. A candy bar might seem like a small thing, but when handled right, it's a whopping life lesson your son won't forget.

#2: Say what you mean and mean what you say.

Most kids are trained on the 1, 2, 3 principle.

1: "Okay, Gerald, breakfast is ready. Come and get it."
2: "Gerald Timothy, I *said* breakfast is ready. Get in here, or it'll get cold!"
3: "Gerald Timothy Davis, are you not listening to me? Get in here now. It's breakfast time!"

Well, yes, he was listening. He was listening for something specific: for you to raise your voice to the appropriate high pitch with the accompanying use of all three of his names. Then he knew he better pay attention or else there would be consequences. You see, that kid has it timed for how long he can play his computer game until you really are serious and mean business.

But what would happen if you just said what you meant and meant what you said?

"Gerald, breakfast is ready. Come and get it."

Either the kid shows or he doesn't. If he dawdles in half an hour later, his oatmeal is sitting in a cold, congealed mess in that bowl. Yum, appetizing.

Let him figure out what to do with it. You don't warm it up for him. You don't offer to make it fresh or make him anything else. In fact, you're MIA from that kitchen.

You think maybe that kid will act on your first command next time? It's a lot more likely. And if he doesn't, he gets take two on that congealed oatmeal. Natural consequences reign when you say what you mean and mean what you say.

#3: Don't ask questions.

Kids hate questions as much as husbands do, especially when they're asked by well-meaning parents prying into their business. Hatred of questions increases even more in middle school and high school, where kids are trying to figure out who they are separate from Mom, Dad, and big brother or big sister, and where they fear something worse than death: social embarrassment. They don't need a protective mom or dad marching to school to solve their problems for them.

When your kid looks like a thundercloud, if you ask a question, he'll be like a ship with the hatches battened down. No way will you get any information.

Instead, a comment like this is appropriate: "Looks like you had a rough day. If you ever want to talk about anything, let me know. Track me down and I'll be happy to listen to what you're thinking."

When that kid does track you down—for some, it might be later that night or even in a couple of weeks—then do what you said. Listen. Don't offer solutions. Don't solve the problem for him. You'll learn far more that way than you will if you're trying to extract information or fix the problem.

When you do need to show engagement and empathy, comments like these help:

"Mmm, I see."
"I get it. That is rough."
"Wow, I understand."

When you have a problem, what's the first thing you want? An empathetic listener. Oftentimes you know what you want to do, but you simply need to process. Having support gives you the courage to stand back up after being knocked down. Then you can move confidently ahead with your game plan.

A healthy child doesn't want to be rescued. He wants to solve the problem with his own brains, brawn, and skills. He merely needs you, the one he trusts most, to have his back and listen to his problem, processing, and plan.

> **A healthy child doesn't want to be rescued. He wants to solve the problem with his own brains, brawn, and skills.**

Depending on his temperament, your child may need a few complaining sessions first. If all you're hearing is complaints, though, this type of parental response is helpful: "That's indeed a problem. I get why you're concerned. But I know you. You'll figure it out. You always do."

Then you go on to give an example of where your child was in a tough spot, handled it well, and got back on his feet. That'll put a smile back on his face and empower him to do what he needs to do in this situation too.

#4: Act, don't react.

It takes two to tango, and you don't have to do the dance. It's hard to keep a fight going if you're the only one in it.

Let's say your fifth grader has a science fair project due tomorrow. She's waited until the last minute, and now her volcano isn't spewing smoke like it's supposed to.

"It's all your fault," she yells at you. "You told me this would be a good science project."

> *Strike 1:* She's got you there. She's speaking the truth. You did suggest this one because you were frustrated with her not acting. In fact, you looked up some projects on your own, and this one looked simple.

Now you have a choice. You could go on to these:

Strike 2: "Well, I told you to try it a few times to make sure it worked. But you chose to wait until the last minute. That's all on you."

Strike 3: "Don't you dare make me responsible for *your* science project."

Or you could stop after her first strike and be the adult. Engaging in the tango by giving your hotheaded little missy the facts won't get you anywhere. It'll only provoke a worse fight, and then you're the one who'll feel bad.

Instead, count to 10 before you open your mouth. Then say in a straightforward tone, "Well, I'm sure you'll figure it out." Turn and exit that room.

Let her continue that solo dance on your kitchen floor. What she does next is all up to her. Even if she has a momentary hissy fit, she'll soon realize nobody is going to rescue her. You might want to clue in any siblings not to help.

If she gets an F on that project, let her teacher do the talking instead of you. A dose of responsibility and accountability is just what the doctor ordered.

When you do open your mouth—you are human, after all—and know a second later that you've inserted your foot, own up to it:

- "I'm sorry."
- "I didn't know what I was talking about in that situation, and I jumped in too quickly."
- "I was really off base in what I said to you. You didn't deserve that."
- "Will you tell me what you wanted to tell me again? I'll make sure to listen this time."

When you own up to your failures, you role-model critical life lessons for your child:

- If you mess up, admit it.
- Say you're sorry.
- Choose to do the right thing the next time.
- Allow life to move on.

#5: *Learn how to deflect arguments.*

Your tenth grader wants to go on a two-day backpacking trip in the wild with two guys from his class this summer. You know he hates hiking and bugs and likely won't do well in a tent even for one night.

Your sixth grader thinks you're from the Stone Age since you won't allow her to have a social media account. She says all the other kids have one.

Your artistic second grader decides to paint her new backpack the night before school starts since she's aiming for a new look. Problem is, paint needs time to dry, and it needs to dry flat.

Your four-year-old insists he wants fish sticks for dinner because he saw them on a TV commercial. You know he can't stand anything that remotely resembles fish.

When friction starts to mount, use these three helpful methods:

The surprise argument deflector.

Want to stop any arguments before they start? Say, "You could be right" in response to any statement or curveball thrown your way.

This surprising technique works especially well with a teenager who is poised for a fight. Rebutting your child's statement sets you both up for a standoff. But acknowledging her perspective opens the door for her to explain more about what she meant. It may be exactly what you were thinking, not at all what you were thinking, or way better or worse than what you were thinking.

When your kids are busily preparing their next missile, your statement will blow 'em right out of the water and leave them openmouthed.

Try it. Let the fun begin.

The escape clause.

This is the perfect technique for buying time to think through your response. Say, "That's an interesting idea. Tell me more about that."

This encourages the child to share with you what she's really thinking, if the idea is important to her. If it's merely a wild statement thrown out there to see how you'll react, that will become clear too. She won't have any facts or research to back up her statement.

After you've heard her out, say, "Let me think on that" or "I'll get back to you on that."

Parents who use that method skip reacting to about 95 percent of the cockamamie ideas their kids toss their way. Why? Because if they wait 24 hours, the kids are onto a new idea.

If the idea persists, then go for round two: "I understand you're very interested in that. Tell me more."

Again, you're engaging with your child without saying yes or no. You can always grant in fantasy what you can't in reality by entertaining her ideas, research, and imagination. It doesn't mean you have to agree to do what she wants.

Say nothing, do nothing.

There are times in every parent's life when saying and doing nothing is the best option. When you're about to blow, turn your back and walk away. Some words are better not said, and some actions are better left undone. There will be a better time and place for you to get a point across when you are in control of your emotions.

The Leman take. How would I deflect arguments in the four situations listed above?

For the wannabe outdoorsy type, I'd use *the escape clause*: "That's an interesting idea. Tell me more about that."

He can wax philosophical about what he and the guys are talking about.

You entertain the ideas and then say casually, "I went camping once. I remember it was very dark at night, and there were lots of bugs. Then again, I'm sure you could adjust."

"It's that dark? How many bugs are there?" your startled son says, as if the idea of critters in the great outdoors is a revolutionary concept.

"I'm sure you've done all the research yourself. If you want to share anything with me, I'm all ears."

If that boy really hates the dark, bugs, and hiking, he'll be rethinking that trip. If not, you might want to suggest he pack some bug spray.

For the social media entrepreneur, I'd use *the surprise argument deflector*: "You might be right. Maybe I am from the Stone Age." Then you walk away.

When she asks you about it later, and she will, you use *the escape clause* to find out why she wants a social media account: "Tell me more about that."

She'll tell you everybody else has one and that it's cool how many likes you can get, etc.

You nod. "I see. So . . . everybody at school gets lots of likes."

"Well, no, you have to work to get likes, and that shows how popular you are," she tells you excitedly.

"Oh, I get it," you say nonchalantly. "Then if you get likes, you're popular. If you don't get likes, or don't get as many likes as somebody else, then kids gossip about you. Ah, I see."

That ought to give some food for thought.

For the artistic second grader, I'd say *nothing, do nothing*. That second grader makes her own choice the next morning. Either she takes that sticky backpack to school, even if it looks like something the cat dragged in, or she becomes a master at juggling pencils, crayons, notepaper, Kleenex, and whatever else is required the first day of school. Or she might surprise you and get creative with a plastic bag. But let the solution be *her* idea and decision, not yours.

For the gullible kid who believes every food on commercials tastes good, I'd use the *escape clause* first: "Tell me why you're interested in fish sticks."

After his explanation, indulge him, but not for dinner that night. Even preschoolers need to learn some patience. The next time you go to the grocery store, if he is still asking for fish sticks, buy a small pack. Bake those fish sticks in the oven and *say nothing*. Serve them with a flourish, with no warning of "I don't think you're going to like these."

Let the surprise on his face be your entertainment for the evening.

#6: Ask for their input.

If you've been a calling-the-shots parent or a do-everything-for-your-kids parent, it's time to reinvent your parenting style and do something entirely foreign to you: ask for your child's opinion. Yes, I know, that's radical thinking.

But, after all, you're reading this book because *something* prompted you to. You want to raise a successful child in a "whatever" world. And many of you want a few things to change around your house.

If you want a successful child, grow their positive character traits. Don't do things for them that they should do for themselves. Instead of telling them what to do, ask what they think. Instead of controlling, commit yourself to listening. Instead of making demands, solicit suggestions.

The [Your Last Name] Poll

Ever heard of the Gallup poll? People love to share their opinions. Your kids do too. In fact, they can't resist it. So why not create your own poll at home? The family fridge is a great spot for it since everybody has to eat sometime. Or you can start a poll on a shared Google Drive or other private media account.

Try a tantalizing title like, "What I Wish Mom and Dad Knew," and within seconds, those blanks will be filled by even the most reticent teenager.

- I really hate _____.
- It makes me mad when _____.
- It's unfair when _____.
- I miss _____.
- What I wish we'd do as a family is _____.
- My favorite time of day is _____
- The time I feel the most loved is _____.

Note that this survey moves from negative emotions to positive emotions, so that grievances can be aired but family members exit with happier memories.

To address specific issues and get even quiet family members' opinions, you could offer options.

- The best way to spend a Saturday morning is:
  __sleeping in
  __eating pancakes
  __coffee with Dad
  __reading books with Mom

- The kind of vacation I wish we'd go on:
  __playing in the water
  __hiking in the mountains
  __having s'mores in our own backyard

- What makes me feel most loved:
  __time alone with Dad/Mom
  __having friends over
  __getting a present
  __someone telling me I'm good at something

Training Your Kid "Up"

For those of you who like pithy proverbs or are people of faith, Proverbs 22:6 says, "Train up a child in the way he should go: and when he is old, he will not depart from it."[4] Sounds like a simple directive and then a promise, doesn't it?

But consider this. Authoritarian parents tend to use that verse like a club over their children. Here's their thinking: "There is a specific way you *should* go, and I know the best way. I'm the parent, after all. If you do as I say, things will go well for you. But cross me and it's my responsibility to make sure you adhere to the way I say you should go."

Instead of training "up" their children by expecting the best from them, they are training them "down" by expecting them to go against their parents, threatening them with ensuing action *when* they do, not *if* they do, and giving them no opportunity for growth in their own choices.

Permissive parents focus on the "up" part of the verse. Here's their thinking: "I want my children to have happy lives, so I need to train them to be happy. I must always praise them and keep them from feeling bad. If they aren't happy, that will mean I've failed as a parent, and I'll feel bad."

Such parents are always worried about their children's happiness. But, again, are *you* always happy? Then why should your kids be? Being unhappy here and there is a good life lesson that not everything will go their way. When it doesn't, they need tenacity, courage, and balance to deal with that adversity. By wanting your kids to always be "up"—happy, top achievers, never uncomfortable, just rollin' along smoothly on life's highway—you rob them of the chance to experience normal downturns in the safety of your home.

The best life insurance you can purchase for each child is your unswerving commitment to help them develop a healthy self-image: one in which they and others are equally important but play differing roles. That means you can't be a doormat or the martyr who lives only for your children. You need to be the role model who shows what a balanced life is like: taking time for others, taking time for yourself.

Authoritative parents see enough food for thought in the above verse to last a lifetime. The word *train* connotes intention and discipline. You don't try parenting techniques willy-nilly until you fall into one that temporarily works. Instead you actively teach and role-model as you walk alongside your child day to day. It isn't a one-shot deal. It's a continual process from the time your child enters your home until he spreads his wings and leaves your nest.

You train "up" by encouraging that child to develop key character qualities like courage, endurance, honesty, and tenacity that will serve him well. You provide plenty of affirmation and take hold of the steering wheel when you need to, in order to keep your child safe from the world's clutches. But you don't tightly grasp that steering wheel on your own. Instead, as your child grows, you allow him to put his hand *with* yours on it. Then, by the time he's ready to leave your home, you can let go of the wheel and let him drive that car without you, knowing you've prepared him as well as you possibly can.

Note that phrase "in the way he should go." It doesn't say "in the way *you think* he should go." Every child in your family will have their own bent. Authoritative parents know their kids may not turn out like them and likely won't, but they enjoy the ride along the way of finding out what that child will become.

When you allow your kids to discover and explore their own talents and support them in that mission, the friction in your house is a lot less. Yes, you'll all still have different personalities and your own quirks. But you as the parent won't be engaging in a fruitless, aggravating activity anymore: trying to force your square-peg child into your round-peg hole.

That's a win-win for both of you.

STRATEGY #8

KEEP THE RELATIONSHIP FIRST, ALWAYS

They don't care what you know until they know that you care.

I stumbled upon a Little League game recently when I was out for a walk. Since I'm a baseball player from way back, I thought, *Oh, this'll be fun*, and stopped to watch.

As I was standing next to the cage, a ground ball got hit out to center field. For those of you who don't understand baseball, a ground ball can be a grand slam. It's rare, but it can happen when three bases are loaded with runners, and this ultimate hit scores four runs, the most runs possible in one play.

But in this case I noticed something strange. The ball was aimed at the center fielder, but he was crouched down on all fours.

That kid's parents were directly behind me in the cheering section. They started yelling, "Michael! Michael, get the ball. It's right there, Michael."

He was still on all fours staring at the ground. Finally he looked up and yelled, "I'm looking for a four-leaf clover."

His parents stared at each other for a split second.

Mom shrugged. Dad eyed the reactions of the angry parents on either side of him. "This is not the time to look for a four-leaf clover," he yelled back at the kid. "This is the time to play *baseball*, so get to it!"

But to that kid, there was nothing more important at that moment than looking for a four-leaf clover.

That wasn't the only thing amiss about that game.

Within minutes of that incident, three kids came running to the sidelines since there were more than three outfielders. "Coach, can we sit?" they asked.

"You know the rules," the coach replied. "Look on the tree there." He pointed. "Line up according to batting order."

Kid #1: "I don't want to hit. I want to sit."

Kid #2: "No, *I* want to sit."

Kid #3: "No, *I* get to sit first."

Soon all three kids were in each other's faces, fighting over who could sit first.

This was the top of the first inning. The game had just started. I shook my head. Why were these kids even playing baseball?

But I already knew the answer: because their parents wanted them to. Getting on the fast track of success meant signing those kids up to play baseball, even if they'd rather sit or search for a four-leaf clover in the field.

Kids Need to Be Kids

Parenting isn't easy, but it is simple. It requires you to be the adult so that your child can be the child.

Yet many parents tend to want to hurry kids in the growing-up process. We sign up for kindergarten academies when babies are still in the womb. Tykes are hurried off to preschool, a second-language academy, Toddler Technical Institute, or Urchin University. After all, we're eager to help our kids get a good start in life. We even have graduations from preschool for four-year-olds.

Why all this flurry? Because we're afraid our kids will miss the success train if we don't jump on it early and schedule them for a horde of activities. However, if we're only SUV drivers, shuttling our kids from activity A to activity B, we're missing connecting with their hearts.

My advice? Let your *kids* choose one activity per semester. You don't sign her up for piano lessons or him up for T-ball. Each child makes a choice and is accountable for it. If you have more than one child, one activity per child is more than enough for you to keep track of anyway.

We Lemans had five kids. Without that rule of one activity per semester, we'd have been ships passing in the night.

Some families, like the Linders, who don't have any extra cash to spare, choose activities even more creatively. Each summer they raise money through various family activities, including cleaning others' yards and making frozen meals. At the beginning of the new school year, they split the cash between their two kids, who can choose either to fund an activity for a semester at school or to put it toward a special purchase.

The point is, you say no to all activities per child except for one. Once your child makes her choice, it's a done deal. If she hates what she chose, she does it for that semester anyway. It doesn't matter whether she's 7 or 12; next time she'll choose more carefully. Meanwhile, she learns the hard lesson of having to carry through on her responsibility for something she chose but doesn't enjoy. Believe me, there will be lots of those times later in life. The sooner she learns about it, the better.

Other perks include less time for you running from point A to point B. With less stress, your buttons aren't pushed as easily. You can have relaxed family dinners with stimulating discussions. Siblings have more time together to rub off their rough edges and learn how to get along. You might even be able to take that dream family vacation instead of spending money on gas for that SUV.

> Never sacrifice what is most important: time together. No gadget or toy can make up for Mommy's and Daddy's attention.

Many parents tell me they've sacrificed greatly to give their kids the best opportunities in life. Yes, all parents do that. However, never sacrifice what is most important: time together. No gadget or toy can make up for Mommy's and Daddy's attention.

If You Care, They Will Cooperate

Things about your kids may drive you crazy, and things about you may drive them crazy. No two humans will get along perfectly 24/7. But a wise parent takes the high road, acts like the adult in the situation, and keeps the long-term relationship in mind.

A wise coach I know, who's sent tons of college players to the NFL, said it best: "They don't care what you know until they know that you care." Or, put another way, no kid in his right mind will listen to what you say until he knows you're in his court.

Success isn't a solo enterprise. In today's "all about me" culture, those who look for opportunities to encourage others, walk alongside them in mentoring, and invest in multiple ways in their lives will stand out from the typical pack.

Your kids need you not only to be a parent but to be part of their life team of loyal, trustworthy people who won't leave their side no matter what happens. Those people allow them to grow and change, tell them the truth in a straightforward manner when needed, and genuinely encourage them as they invent their own paths.

Do the following four things, and your child will have no doubt you're in his court.

#1: Choose your words wisely.

The words you choose to use and the tones with which you say them have everything to do with how willing your child is to listen. Caring means getting behind your child's eyes, glimpsing the way he views the world, and developing a heart-to-heart relationship that uniquely connects with him. Your relationship with that child and the roles he perceives he has in your family have a great deal to do with his performance in all other areas. So don't major on the minors.

My artistic daughter Lauren has had just about every color of hair on the planet. One time when she was trying to find parking to meet up with me, I joked with her, "Just look for the blue-hair lot." You see, down the road, it won't matter that she has blue hair. By then, she'll have a different color or be back to her au naturel. What matters is that she and I maintain a good relationship as father and daughter.

How well do you communicate with your kids? Do you think before you speak when they lob surprises your way? Do you keep your mouth shut when you don't know what to say? Do you connect with your kids only when you have to—to give them information or chide them for doing something wrong—or do you actively work to connect with them and their interests in unforgettable, tangible ways?

Most of all, now that you know what each child needs and wants most from you, how will you craft your technique to specifically suit that child?

#2: Practice the ABCs.

One of the saddest comments I've ever read in a newspaper was from a 17-year-old. When he saw the state prison in Florence, Arizona, and knew he was heading through its gates to stay there awhile, he said it was the most beautiful sight in the world.

Dr. Leman's 10-Second Solutions

Q: We're worried about our middle-school son. Who he is seems to switch from day to day, depending on the latest trends and what his peers say or do. How can we turn him back into the kid we used to know and who liked hanging out with us?

A: Kids are chameleons, especially at that age. They'll try on lots of different skin colors, sometimes wanting to shock and other times wanting to blend in to avoid being eaten by others in the school jungle.

Thankfully, most of the stages that drive you nuts don't last very long. Keep an eye on your kid's heart, not the latest trends in hair or fashion or even the latest music craze.

But you need to realize something else. Your child will never be who he used to be. He's growing up. He now has friends he wants to hang with. That's all very normal. He's enlarging his world beyond your tight family circle, as he should. He may not want his parents to hug him or call him "Stevie" in front of his friends anymore, because such an act is embarrassing to a boy trying to become a man. He might want Dad, who drives a beat-up truck, to drop him off a block or two from school because his peers make fun of his ride.

This is the time when you retain your sense of humor, and you don't allow the small things to get to you. That kid does still like to hang out with you, but you'll have to work harder at connecting.

Don't assume he wants to do the same things he did when he was a little kid. Instead of snuggling up next to you on the couch to watch a cartoon like he used to on Saturday morning, he might want to catch some extra z's and then an action thriller in the late afternoon instead. He might want popcorn and coffee instead of the Cheetos and orange soda he loved as a treat when he was younger. Playing catch in the backyard might transform into a tailgating party at a local football game.

Being an adult means you should be the adaptable one. After all, that kid already has enough body changes going on to keep him busy, not to mention mounting homework and that jungle of peers.

I was stunned. What kind of family did that kid come from that he thought prison was better than home? Certainly not a loving, supportive one. His mom had tried to do her best but was deeply troubled. His father had taken off early in his life. There was so much dysfunction in his extended family that no one much cared about the kid. School had also chewed him up and spit him out.

In short, no one accepted that boy. He had nowhere to belong except in a gang, which is what got him in trouble. No one faced off with him, like that teacher did with me my senior year of high school, and told him he was unique, had skills, or could be competent at anything.

That kid was completely on his own in a tough world. No wonder he thought prison, where at least he'd get food, a roof over his head, and some people to hang out with, was a good deal better than where he'd come from.

All kids crave to be accepted, to know they belong somewhere, and to be considered competent. If they don't find those things in your home, they'll go searching for them, like that 17-year-old did.

A: *Acceptance*

A lot of kids don't feel accepted because they're different from the rest of the family. Maybe everybody in the family is athletic except for them. Their only athletic achievement is managing to hit the birdie once in a badminton game in the backyard. But different is not good or bad; it's just different. In fact, if two people are exactly alike, then one of them is unnecessary.

When your kids feel accepted by you, they will feel loved and cared for, even when you don't agree on something. Little expressions go a long way.

Recently I walked into an elementary school lunchroom and was immediately surrounded by about 60 kids. I made sure to comment on something about every child, whether a pretty hair ribbon or a beautiful smile. Taking time to build a relationship with each child says, "I accept you as you, just as you are. I'm glad you're in this world. You make it better by being in it."

B: *Belonging*

Try this experiment at home if you have young children. Go into the kitchen and hug your spouse. Within 4.6 seconds, torpedoes will speed out from all directions toward you and zero in on your location. They will come right up between you.

Why? Well, because children are the enemy.

No, seriously, they do that because they want to be a part of your loving union. Kids want to belong, even if they don't want to admit that to you when they're in the hormone group.

My daughter Krissy was a volleyball player, and her first game was an away one. The previous night she'd announced at the dinner table, "I don't want any of you coming."

As the father, I touted my authority and announced, "Krissy, I'm gonna be there."

"If you come," my 15-year-old fired back, "you better not yell."

You see, I knew my daughter very well. She was excited and nervous about that game. She needed some backup from the family, even if she said she wanted to go it solo.

The game was 90 miles away. I quietly rearranged my work schedule and a couple of other activities to get there. When I arrived, the game had just begun. There was Krissy Leman, out there in her set position with her hands on her knees.

I was a good 75 feet away when I saw her left hand move. It was the smallest of finger movements up and down a couple of times to acknowledge, "Dad, I see you here."

At that moment I was glad I had moved heaven and earth to be at that game. And I kept my promise. I didn't yell, as hard as it was for a baby of the family not to do so.

Whether your child succeeds in life has everything to do with your family life at home. As the old saying goes, "If you see a turtle on a fence post, he didn't get there by himself." Your kids can't go it alone. They need you.

We also had a saying in the Leman home when my kids were growing up: "I'm a Leman." What exactly did that mean? My kids joke that they weren't sure, but they lived by it then and have ever since. Whenever they faced a tough situation and told me about it later, they'd say, "Dad, I remembered what you always say: 'You're a Leman.'"

It meant that because they belong to this family and have the character traits of this family, they would do what a Leman would do in that situation. If kindness was required, they would be kind. If someone was in need, they would be generous. If someone was being hurt in any way, they would step in to help.

When you develop character traits you all live by as a family, you build a firm foundation that can't be shaken. By the end of this book, you'll have your own list of traits solidified. You'll be able to say to your kids, "Remember, you're a [your last name]," and your child will instinctively know what you mean.

Yes, you might get smirks, sighs, or those ubiquitous eye-rolls, but don't let them fool you. Your kids are secretly very glad to be part of your family. It's their comfort zone and safety net from which they can confidently explore.

Kids crave belonging. If they can't belong to you, they'll find somewhere else to belong. In a "whatever" world, that's a scary possibility indeed.

C: Competence

Last year I went to see a play at the Leman Academy of Excellence and was happily surprised to find out the director of the play was an enterprising seventh grader. The skillful teacher who headed up that *Annie* musical decided to do three different performances, switching off the lead characters so more than one student got to play the same role. Though adults helped make costumes, all the principals of the play—stage manager, lighting, audio—were positions filled by students (we call them "scholars"). Talk about training in action.

Your children need to know that you believe they are competent to carry out their tasks well. You don't just expect them to do the minimum to get by; you expect them to embrace their roles and do it with gusto, like those kids in *Annie*.

Kids whose parents expect them to be competent will, 99 percent of the time, be competent. However, competency starts with responsibility and accountability. Start with small decisions, allow consequences to freely reign, and your child will grow in competence.

Think of it this way. If you haven't painted a room before, you might be a bit uncomfortable tackling that for the first time. But once you've painted one room, you've gained in competence. *I got this. It wasn't so hard after all.* You start eyeing the rest of the house. *I think I could tackle the rest of the place now. One room every weekend until it's done.*

That's how your belief in your child's competence works.

The 10 Best Parental Practices

1. Shut up and listen unless you're asked for advice.
2. Don't ask questions. Say, "Tell me more about that."
3. Lavish time, attention, and affection on your kids (just not in front of their friends).
4. Make time together count.
5. Show interest in their interests.
6. Grant in fantasy what you can't in reality.
7. Treat each of your kids differently.
8. Tell stories about dumb things you did when you were growing up.
9. Don't major on the minors. Life will go on, despite any evidence to the contrary.
10. Keep your sense of humor.

#3: Encourage, don't praise.

There's a mountain of difference between encouragement and praise. Encouragement focuses on an event or task done well. Praise focuses on an individual.

Encouragement says, "It must feel great to study hard and then get a good result." Praise says, "You're so smart. You're smarter than anybody else in the class. I knew you'd get a good grade."

Encouragement says, "What a beautiful horse drawing. I know you've been researching how to draw them online. Good for you for going the extra mile to figure that out." Praise says, "Oh, look! Junior drew a horse. Isn't that just the most precious, perfect horse? Oh, Frank! Come look. It's the best horse ever. We'll have to show Grandma and the neighbors."

See the difference?

There's a chasm between the two, and your child knows it. He knows he's not the smartest in the class, nor is his drawing perfect. He also knows he's not the best ever at anything. There are other kids who are better than him.

Don't try to fool your child, but do reward his efforts through encouraging them. A child who feels the internal success of knowing he did something well will always outshine in the long term the child who was falsely praised and rewarded.

The sweetest words to a child's heart are, "I care about you. I believe in you. I have confidence in you." Encouraging statements like, "Wow, you figured that out on your own. I love seeing you digging into a project and finishing it with a flair. That has to feel great inside," will powerfully motivate your child to do more of the same and tackle even bigger projects.

And don't forget that encouragement doesn't only have to come via verbal affirmation. Try something old-fashioned this week: the power of the handwritten note. Children of all ages love to get mail or surprise messages tucked into lunches or backpacks.

Such expressions go a long way toward winning your child's heart and cooperation.

#4: Laugh every day.

Laughter is an essential ingredient to a well-rounded child. It's like sprinkling water on a growing plant, then adding sunshine to boot. Laughing *together* (note: not at each other, which is hurtful and erects barriers) gels families and solves disputes faster than any other method.

The family that laughs together stays together and wants to play together now and in the future. My family is living proof. With five kids and four grandchildren scattered across the US, we still get together every chance we can. When we do, our laughter rings off the walls. We do our best to include anyone around us too, whether servers in restaurants or a lonely older person on a park bench as we pass by. Even via text and phone, there's not a day that we don't laugh together still.

No matter how intense a day is, you can always find one thing to laugh about. Laughter really is the best medicine, so lighten up.

Knowing Your Kid as Well as Your Own Smell

You can learn a lot about parenting from movies. Trust me, I know.

Take the crazy, classic movie *The Three Amigos*. Have you ever seen it? If not, then you're missing out . . . though my classy wife would beg to differ. She can't understand how I can watch that cheesy 1980s movie over and over and still laugh. Then again, it includes one of my all-time favorite lines: "I know each of you like I know my own smell."[1]

As you seek to rear your kids into successful adults, that should be your goal: to know each of your children as intimately as you know your own smell.

When my kids were growing up, I used to bring them a special treat every Friday. But every single treat was different, because each of my kids liked something different. For my daughter Hannah, it was an éclair.

Hannah is now a mom of twin girls, Ezra and Olive. When they'd just turned four, Hannah bought them chocolate éclairs and took cute pictures of them with chocolate-smeared faces to send to Grandma and Grandpa. She told the girls, "When I was little, my dad brought me an éclair every Friday morning."

Ezra popped up out of her chair and yelled, "Amen!"

The legacy continues. You see how important little things are? Because I knew Hannah like I knew my own smell, I brought her an éclair. Now she's passing on the chocolaty blessing to her own kids. Each time she does, she feels the warmth of her daddy's love all over again from the memory of that treat when she was growing up.

Each of your kids is an original. He's not a cheap print you buy in a department store that's cranked out on an assembly line. She's not a facsimile copy. Originals take time, care, and patience.

Each child will view the world through the lenses of birth order and their own experiences and will respond differently to the same parental tactics. That's why the worst thing you can do is treat your kids the same. Do that and you'll grow resentful children who can't wait to exit your home as soon as possible.

When you know your child as well as you know your own smell, and you respond to situations in light of all you know about that particular child, you won't react and be sorry for it later. You won't make as many missteps. And when you do, you'll be an adult and be the first to say, "I'm sorry. I was wrong. Please forgive me."

You won't push her to grow up fast, because you know that happens too swiftly anyway. That baby you walked the floor with all night to get her to sleep is now walking down the aisle for her high-school graduation.

You'll win her cooperation through role-modeling and caring. You'll practice the ABCs to ensure your child knows that she is accepted by you, that she belongs to your family, and that you believe she is competent. You'll encourage her but not falsely praise her. And every day, you'll laugh together.

That, parents, is the recipe for life success, and you already have all the ingredients in your back pocket.

Dr. Leman's 10-Second Solutions

Q: My 15-year-old doesn't seem to care about anyone other than himself. How can I teach him that others matter too? Like his sister and the elderly lady next door who needs help with her groceries or getting her mail?

A: All those things you do for him, like making him snacks, cleaning up after him, and washing his undies? Stop doing them. Right now. A lack of easy-to-access food and aromatic clothes are good motivators for change. Eventually, he'll have to ask, "What gives? Why did you stop doing laundry? What's wrong with you?"

You shrug. "There's nothing wrong with me. But there's something wrong with you. You don't seem to care about anyone other than yourself. You don't say thank you for things I do for you. You walk by Mrs. Eldridge when she's tugging her grocery cart up the walkway. Since you choose not to help others, I'm choosing not to help you."

Then you pivot and walk away from your very confused, jaw-dropped teenager, who is going to have a lot to ponder.

Let the games begin.

Taking the Long View

My dear wife, Sande, loves to send me to the store. I think it's one of her many callings in life.

Whenever she asks, I go, like a dutiful husband. I even make fun out of it. Once when I was standing in a long checkout line and people were looking bored, I said loudly, "I'll tell you how much my wife doesn't like me. She sent me here, to Costco, on the day before Thanksgiving." The whole line of grouchy customers lightened up and started laughing.

But seriously, my wife loves to send me on missions. Some of them should be called "mission impossible." Recently she sent me to a big home store to buy Miracle-Gro for feeding outdoor flowers.

The weathered guy at the help counter scratched his chin. "Well, you can check down that aisle." He pointed. "But I don't think we have any root stimulant now. That's for planting season, in the spring."

It was early November.

Why did my beloved wife, whom I affectionately call Mrs. Uppington for her precise, firstborn ways, send me there at that time? She well knew that any flowers she planted now would die. We live in Arizona, along a riverbed where it gets extremely cold at night. But she was planting the flowers anyway.

Me? I'm too stupid to remember season to season that planting in November doesn't work. I just follow what my wife tells me to do. So I dutifully went to three stores: Ace Hardware, Walmart, and Lowe's. All were the bearer of the same bad news: no Miracle-Gro.

On the way home, I realized how familiar the refrain was and how crazy I was to fall for it. Then I laughed to myself.

At least I'd convinced Mrs. Uppington a while back that she couldn't grow citrus trees in our front yard, so I was a step ahead there. Especially since citrus trees aren't cheap. Now I had to start working on the "flowers die in the fall" concept.

But her tenacity was admirable. She had a game plan in mind. She wanted the yard and house to look lovely with flowers when all our kids came home for Thanksgiving and Christmas. That's one of the many reasons I love and respect that woman. No matter what, making things beautiful for our family times together—whether flowers outdoors, a festive table centerpiece, special menus—is part of her winning attitude about life.

With that game plan in mind, then, is it really a big deal for me to go the extra mile and sweep the front steps and porch to make her happy? Or to simply smile about her enthusiasm instead of grumbling about spending a few shekels on flowers?

Have you ever seen a really beautiful garden? People who have green thumbs, like Sande, amaze people with black thumbs like me. Besides enjoying being surrounded by lovely blooms, I've learned a few things too.

A watched, hovered-over, late-blooming flower will never bloom with too much watering or smothering. It will merely become limp and have the inability to stand up under harsh conditions. A plant that isn't watered with affection, isn't given a dose of Miracle-Gro for encouragement every once in a while, and is merely treated to the harshest sunlight and heat will wither and die.

Plants and flowers are a lot like children. They need consistent watering and feeding in order to thrive. The one they most need those from is you, the master gardener in their lives.

When you love and respect your kids, you'll go along with their quirky gestures that may seem silly or misplaced but mean a lot to them.

You'll dream with them. "You want to be the first person to live on Mars? Well, I wonder what that would be like, don't you? What do you think?" Who knows? You may be growing a future planetary scientist in your home.

You'll grant in fantasy what you can't in reality. Your child wants an iguana and you live in Alaska. Why not role-play having one, using a stuffed animal and your imagination? Perhaps down the road the online research your curious child did on animals may lead him to become a veterinarian or a zoologist.

Spend time exploring your children's interests, whether it's stacking colored cups, growing an ant farm, or exploring indie music online.

And you might even help plant some flowers outside in late fall just because they're pretty and important to the one you love.

CONCLUSION

Paying It Forward

> *Why your legacy of success keeps on giving.*

All of us have parental moments where we realize we've done something good along the way, in spite of any mistakes we've made. Here's a flashback journey to one of my moments.

I spend a lot of time on planes, flying to speak with groups of people across the US and Canada. When my daughter Krissy was in college in Chicago, I'd try to time my stopovers there to have a few minutes to pop by and see her on the fly.

On one of those jaunts, I stopped by her school. Since I knew her schedule, I headed for the anatomy classroom and stood outside the door.

The door swung open wide at the end of class. Students started flocking out and stared at the short, fat, half-balding guy—aka, me—who clearly was not like any of the others.

Krissy came out laughing, surrounded by a college boy and two girls. They were in the midst of a fun conversation.

Still, I was her father. Of course she'd see me.

But she walked right by.

I couldn't believe it. My bulging middle that has had too much pie isn't small, and some students had to do the Watusi to get by me in the narrow hallway.

That's when I decided to do the inexcusable in a young adult's eyes. I bellowed out, in front of those peers, "How are you doing, Leemie?"

Krissy jerked to a halt. She swiveled, spotted me, and started jumping up and down. "My *daddy's here*. My daddy's here. Everybody . . . my daddy's right here," she nearly screamed before running to me and giving me a big hug.

By that time, a few tears were trickling down this dad's face. In the onslaught of such tender emotion, I felt like a wuss.

But you know what? I couldn't wait to call my beloved bride and share with her that life vignette.

That daughter is the same one who told me not to go to her first volleyball game. Yet when I drove those 90 miles and showed up anyway, she gave me that tiny finger acknowledgment on the court. She was happy her daddy came.

Years later, she was thrilled her daddy had gone out of his way to enter her world again.

All the love and time you spend in rearing your children pays off in scenes like that, doesn't it? It's not easy being a parent these days. With school, activities, and the internet, strangers have a profound effect on how kids are being raised. But when *you* invest in your kids, you'll get the biggest payoff in history: their hearts. And your investment doesn't end with your children. Their partner, your grandchildren, and your great-grandchildren will be grateful for your legacy too.

Any transformation in your home starts with you.

Start with the end in mind. Identify the qualities you want your kids to have and go after them.

Expect the best of your characters and make behavioral adjustments along the way.

Give respect and a winning attitude and you'll motivate your kids to fly to the moon.

Be the hero your children want to watch and be like.

Use reality discipline combined with the magic of the three Cs: communication, compassion, and commitment.

Don't let anything distract you from your ultimate goal.

Remember that when you minimize friction, you optimize solutions *and* get your kids to listen.

Above all, keep your relationship paramount. Nothing matters more to your children than knowing you care and are in their court.

Today is a perfect day for a slight tweak of your parenting style or a complete overhaul and a fresh start. You can do it. I believe in you. But, as former secretary of state Colin Powell said, "A dream doesn't become reality through magic; it takes sweat, determination and hard work."[1]

However, when you put your all into parenting and follow the principles and advice in this book, not only will the work be worth it, but you'll look back and say, "That is the best thing I ever did."

BONUS SECTION

Especially for Blended-Family Parents

> *Three big mistakes to avoid so you can blend instead of puree.*

If you're a stepparent or the adoptive parent of an older child and you're reading this book, you have an unprecedented opportunity to influence your child and her road to success.

Following are the top three mistakes you can easily avoid, once you're aware of them.

Mistake #1: Trying to Be "Instant Parent"

Forming a new family doesn't mean you become an instant parent, as much as you might want it to be that way. Your children have had other parents, guardians, or no parents at all. You need to earn their trust, their respect, and the honor of them calling you "Mom" or "Dad." Such a precious label won't come automatically.

All of us have been imprinted by earlier experiences, and childhood memories are complicated. The foundation of a blended family is often cemented with the mortar of anger, bitterness, hurt, and jealousy because of broken relationships, broken promises, abandonment, or death.

For instance, your eight-year-old stepdaughter remembers the balloons from her last birthday party with Mom, the fear when her parents fought late at night, the relief of the truce, then the bitterness when her family was ripped apart by divorce.

Your 15-year-old son has vivid memories of trying to protect you from an abusive ex and suffering for it.

Your five-year-old adopted daughter remembers the moment of deep betrayal and loss when she was abandoned by her birth parent, but she may not have the vocabulary to voice it. She feels nervous if you leave the room.

Your nine-year-old stepson remembers the last time his father played ball in the backyard with him . . . and died minutes later of a heart attack when he was only 38.

Those memories aren't immediately wiped out by switching homes and joining a new family. In addition, nearly everything has changed about those kids' lives. They're living with different people, in a different place, under different rules. If they're older, they may have lost contact with friends or had to change schools. That's a lot of loss for any child to handle.

You be the adult. You do the adjusting.

You be the adult. You do the adjusting. Don't pick on the fact that your child squeezes the toothpaste tube in the middle or leaves hair in the bathroom sink. Or that one child needs a lot of alone time while another loves to vocalize in the garage when she's frustrated.

Instead of trying to become that instant authority figure, work on gently getting to know that child.

- What does she like to eat? What does she do in her free time?

- What makes him feel loved?
- When does he feel most stressed? And when that happens, what's helpful for you to do or not do?
- How does she feel about turning 16 without her birth mom there with her?
- What are his favorite and least favorite times of day? And why?

What's important is that you not ask your child questions or try to extract information. You're not the CIA or the FBI. Instead, if she's foraging through your kitchen, say simply, "I'm guessing you're hungry. I'm hungry too. If there's ever anything you want me to make you, or if you want to cook together, I'd love to do that. Just let me know."

If your adolescent looks grumpy every day after school, don't comment on that. Later, after he's had three huge bowls of cereal as a snack, say, "I noticed that you seem a bit tired after school. I've gotta tell you, it's no wonder you are. I think you're dealing with all the changes around here admirably. When I was 13, I was really grumpy after school. One time I . . ." And you tell a story about your own growing-up years.

That's the way to begin making new connections. No one likes to be forced into a relationship.

One very important note: if you are combining families, whenever there are questions about a specific child or inconsistencies in parenting styles and values, *always* defer to the original parent of that child. That will keep you and your partner rowing the same direction in the same boat, instead of rowing against each other. Otherwise your kids will easily pick up on any division and use it to manipulate you and turn you against each other. As you combine your kids into one household, you'll need to work hard to remain on the same page as parents.

If Mama and Daddy ain't happy, those kiddos will certainly not be happy.

Mistake #2: Assuming Everybody Will Get Along and Insisting They Share Private Spaces

Put two girls, ages 11 and 13 and from two families, into the same bedroom to "bond as sisters," and you'll have DEFCON 3 right in your very own living room.

Kids who have upheavals in their lives need emotional and physical space to adjust. It takes seven years to blend a family. And your goal is to *blend*, not to *puree*. That's why, wherever possible, give each child a room of his or her own, even if that child is in your home only on weekends or holidays.

> It takes seven years to blend a family. And your goal is to *blend*, not to *puree*.

If that means erecting a temporary wall or floor-to-ceiling curtain in a small bedroom, so be it. It will be time and effort well spent. Allow each child to make that space uniquely their own, even if it means you end up with hot pink and hot purple walls in the same bedroom. That says, "I know a lot has changed in your life. But you are still a priority to me and important to this family."

In a blended family, individuals will clash from time to time, but all must treat each other with respect in the midst of addressing concerns. Do your best to be patient, caring, and noncompetitive. Blending families is tricky and requires you to be on your best behavior and to have a long-term perspective. Relationships are based on mutual respect and require time and shared experiences to grow.

Mistake #3: Overindulging to Win Their Affection and Acceptance

It's tempting to shower new members of your family with gifts, but consider this. *Presents* do not equal or trump *presence*. Kids who are in the throes of change desperately need people in their

A Stepparent's 10 Commandments

1. Treat each of your kids differently, according to their unique characteristics, interests, and abilities.
2. Show interest in what they're interested in—school or work, friendships, activities, their beliefs and core values, and most importantly, their ideas and thoughts.
3. Live an exemplary life. Don't tell them how to live; show them.
4. Be gracious and noncompetitive with your partner's ex.
5. Spend one-on-one time with each child, doing something you don't do with any of the other kids.
6. Speak their language, whether through lunch texts, after-school hugs, old-fashioned snail mail (kids *love* getting mail addressed to them), or surprise activities. The little things count greatly.
7. Slip 'em some "money for dreaming on," but keep it small. Don't hover over how they spend it. If one child spends hers on bubble gum and her brother spends his on an iTunes gift card for music, let those be their decisions.
8. Maintain the guidelines and boundaries of the original parent while in the process of meshing your families and coming up with new guidelines that all agree on.
9. Catch your kids doing good and lavish on the encouragement.
10. Look for creative ways to hand down your values and beliefs and create fun.

court who love them. They don't need more stuff. Most of us, in fact, are up to our ears in stuff. Why else do garage sales and repeat boutiques thrive?

Consider this. Kids' interests change rapidly. As they progress age-appropriately, so does the type of toys they're intrigued by. Six months in a young child's life is the difference between those big, fat handheld crayons and the skinnier kind that come in a box. You can't keep up if you're trying to buy their affection.

> You never go wrong showering kids with love, time, and attention balanced with reality discipline.

Why not substitute time with your kids instead? Do an activity that will build memories. You never go wrong showering kids with love, time, and attention balanced with reality discipline.

And here's another thing to consider. If you've adopted a child and have older children, and you lather on the toys to that new-to-your-family member, you'll likely make her siblings jealous. Don't start something that you can't continue for all your children, or you'll have resentment galore crop up down the road.

"Well, you took *her* to Disney World every year, but I only got to go once, since I was in high school by the time she joined our family. You call that fair?"

You don't need such tsunami waves flowing over your home, so keep it simple.

Presence galore, but go light on the presents.

A PARENT'S
TOP 8 WINNING PLAYS

1. Start with the end in mind.
2. Expect the best, get the best.
3. Give and you shall receive.
4. Role-model a disciplined life.
5. Discipline, don't punish.
6. Stay the course.
7. Minimize friction, optimize solutions.
8. Keep the relationship first, always.

NOTES

Strategy #1 Start with the End in Mind

1. 1 Corinthians 13:4–8.
2. Stephen R. Covey, *The 7 Habits of Highly Effective People* (Glencoe, IL: Free Press, 1989), 109.

Strategy #2 Expect the Best, Get the Best

1. Oprah Winfrey, "Michelle Obama Gets Candid with Oprah about Her New Memoir *Becoming*," *O, The Oprah Magazine*, November 12, 2018, https://www .oprahmag.com/entertainment/a24691478/oprah-michelle-obama-becoming -interview/. For more of Michelle Obama's story, read her book *Becoming* (New York: Crown, 2018).
2. Winfrey, "Michelle Obama Gets Candid."
3. Winfrey, "Michelle Obama Gets Candid."
4. Winfrey, "Michelle Obama Gets Candid."
5. Winfrey, "Michelle Obama Gets Candid."
6. Colleen Curry, "Thank You, Michelle Obama: The First Lady's Incredible Legacy," *Global Citizen*, January 17, 2017, https://www.globalcitizen.org/en /content/thank-you-michelle-obama-the-first-ladys-incredibl/.
7. Megan Sims, "Michelle Obama Gets Real about Life after the White House," *The Grio*, February 15, 2020, https://thegrio.com/2020/02/15/michelle-obama -gets-real-about-life-after-the-white-house/.
8. Sims, "Michelle Obama Gets Real."
9. *Evan Almighty*, directed by Tom Shadyac (Universal City, CA: Universal Pictures, 2007), DVD.
10. Ralph Waldo Emerson, *Letters and Social Aims* (Boston: James R. Osgood and Company, 1875), 80.
11. John Wooden, quoted in Craig Impelman, "Be More Concerned with Your Character Than Your Reputation," TheWoodenEffect.com, July 17, 2019,

https://www.thewoodeneffect.com/be-more-concerned-with-your-character
-than-your-reputation/.

Strategy #3 Give and You Shall Receive

1. "Zig Ziglar Quotes," BrainyQuote.com, accessed April 1, 2020, https://
www.brainyquote.com/quotes/zig_ziglar_132266.

Strategy #4 Role-Model a Disciplined Life

1. Kate Taylor, "What Happened to the Students Caught Up in the College
Admissions Scandal?," *New York Times*, February 25, 2020, https://www.nytimes
.com/2020/02/25/us/college-admissions-scandal-students.html.

Strategy #5 Discipline, Don't Punish

1. Anne Ortlund, *Children Are Wet Cement* (Grand Rapids: Revell, 1981).

Strategy #6 Stay the Course

1. William A. Ward, "William A. Ward Quotes," Goodreads, accessed September 23, 2020, https://www.goodreads.com/author/quotes/6207468.William
_A_Ward.

Strategy #7 Minimize Friction, Optimize Solutions

1. "William Henry Harrison," History.com, August 21, 2018, https://www
.history.com/topics/us-presidents/william-henry-harrison#:~:text=Harrison
%E2%80%99s%20Brief%20Presidency%20William%20Henry%20Harrison
%20%281773-1841%29%2C%20America%E2%80%99s,1841%2C%20is%20
the%20shortest%20of%20any%20U.S.%20president.

2. Kevin Leman, *The Birth Order Book: Why You Are the Way You Are* (Grand
Rapids: Revell, 2009).

3. Leman, *Birth Order Book*.

4. KJV.

Strategy #8 Keep the Relationship First, Always

1. *The Three Amigos*, directed by John Landis (Los Angeles, CA: Orion Pictures, 1986), DVD.

Conclusion Paying It Forward

1. "Colin Powell Quotes," BrainyQuote.com, accessed April 1, 2020, https://
www.brainyquote.com/quotes/colin_powell_385927.

ABOUT DR. KEVIN LEMAN

An internationally known psychologist, radio and television personality, speaker, educator, and humorist, **Dr. Kevin Leman** has taught and entertained audiences worldwide with his wit and commonsense psychology.

The *New York Times* bestselling and award-winning author of over 50 titles, including *The Birth Order Book*, *Making Children Mind without Losing Yours*, *Have a New Kid by Friday*, and *Sheet Music*, has made thousands of house calls through radio and television programs, including *FOX & Friends*, Hallmark Channel's *Home & Family*, *The View*, FOX's *The Morning Show*, *Today*, *The 700 Club*, CBS's *The Early Show*, CNN, and *Focus on the Family*. Dr. Leman has served as a contributing family psychologist to *Good Morning America* and frequently speaks to schools, CEO groups, and businesses, including Fortune 500 companies and others such as YPO, Million Dollar Round Table, and Top of the Table.

Dr. Leman's professional affiliations include the American Psychological Association, SAG-AFTRA, and the North American Society of Adlerian Psychology. He received the Distinguished Alumnus Award (1993) and an honorary Doctor of Humane Letters degree (2010) from North Park University; and a bachelor's degree in psychology, and later his master's and doctorate degrees, as well as the Alumni Achievement Award (2003), from the University of Arizona. Dr. Leman is the founder of Leman Academy of Excellence (www.lemanacademy.com).

Originally from Williamsville, New York, Dr. Leman and his wife, Sande, live in Tucson, Arizona, and have five children and four grandchildren.

If you're looking for an entertaining speaker for your event or fundraiser, or for information regarding business consultations, webinars, or the annual "Wit and Wisdom" cruise, please contact:

Dr. Kevin Leman
PO Box 35370
Tucson, Arizona 85740
Phone: (520) 797-3830
Fax: (520) 797-3809
www.birthorderguy.com
www.drleman.com

Follow Dr. Kevin Leman on Facebook (facebook.com/DrKevin Leman) and on Twitter (@DrKevinLeman). Check out the free podcasts at birthorderguy.com/podcast.

Resources by
DR. KEVIN LEMAN

Nonfiction Books for Adults

The Birth Order Book
Have a New Kid by Friday
Why Your Kids Misbehave—and What to Do about It
When Your Kid Is Hurting
Planet Middle School
The Intimate Connection
Sheet Music
Have a New Husband by Friday
Have a New Teenager by Friday
Have a New You by Friday
Have a New Sex Life by Friday
Have a Happy Family by Friday
The Way of the Shepherd (written with William Pentak)
The Way of the Wise
Be the Dad She Needs You to Be
What a Difference a Mom Makes
Parenting the Powerful Child
Under the Sheets

Making Children Mind without Losing Yours
It's Your Kid, Not a Gerbil!
Born to Win
7 Things He'll Never Tell You . . . But You Need to Know
What Your Childhood Memories Say about You
Running the Rapids
Becoming the Parent God Wants You to Be
Becoming a Couple of Promise
A Chicken's Guide to Talking Turkey with Your Kids about Sex (written with Kathy Flores Bell)
First-Time Mom
Step-parenting 101
Living in a Stepfamily without Getting Stepped On
The Perfect Match
Be Your Own Shrink
Stopping Stress before It Stops You
Single Parenting That Works
Why Your Best Is Good Enough
Smart Women Know When to Say No

Fiction: The Worthington Destiny Series, with Jeff Nesbit

A Perfect Ambition
A Powerful Secret
A Primary Decision

Books for Children, with Kevin Leman II

My Firstborn, There's No One Like You
My Middle Child, There's No One Like You
My Youngest, There's No One Like You
My Only Child, There's No One Like You
My Adopted Child, There's No One Like You
My Grandchild, There's No One Like You

DVD/Video Series for Group Use

Have a New Kid by Friday
Making Children Mind without Losing Yours (parenting edition)
Making Children Mind without Losing Yours (public schoolteacher edition)
Value-Packed Parenting
Making the Most of Marriage
Running the Rapids
Single Parenting That Works
Bringing Peace and Harmony to the Blended Family

DVDs for Home Use

Straight Talk on Parenting
Why You Are the Way You Are
Have a New Husband by Friday
Have a New You by Friday
Have a New Kid by Friday

Available at 1-800-770-3830 • www.birthorderguy.com • www.drleman.com

Discover MORE Content from
DR. KEVIN LEMAN

Tune in to his weekly podcast

Have a
New Kid
by Friday
PODCAST

DR. KEVIN LEMAN

Available wherever you get your podcasts

Stop Letting Your Kids
Push Your Buttons

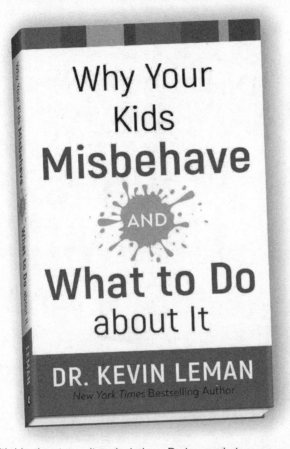

With his signature wit and wisdom, Dr. Leman helps you see through your child's eyes, revealing why they do what they do, who they learn their behaviors from, and why they continue behaving badly. He identifies the stages of misbehavior, where your child is on the spectrum, and how to not only avoid escalating bad behavior but get on the front end and turn it around for good.

No Parent Likes to See
Their Child in Pain

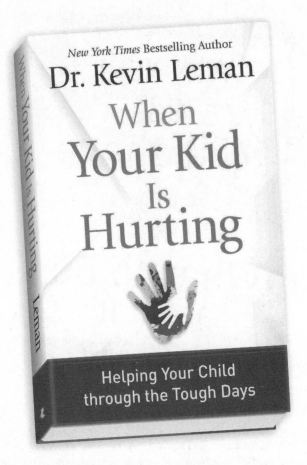

New York Times Bestselling Author
Dr. Kevin Leman

When
Your Kid
Is
Hurting

Helping Your Child
through the Tough Days

But you can navigate even negative events with less drama, more resilience, and a positive attitude. Let Dr. Kevin Leman show you how.

Kid-tested,
parent-approved

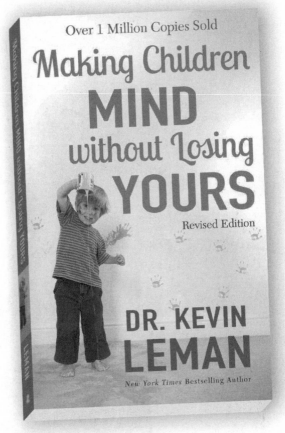

If anyone understands why children behave the way they do, it's Dr. Kevin Leman. In this bestseller he equips parents with seven principles of reality discipline—a loving, no-nonsense parenting approach that really works.